PORTLAND

Dear Portland, Thanks so much for my trip — the most fun I've had in years! Magical, mystical adventure!...

I love your RAINY DRIZZLE!

Bursa Bubbles — you quench my thirst like a fresh rain on a parched desert afternoon!

My Beloved Portland... How I love to lick your creamy center!
E.

One-way streets everywhere! Mikes.

Portland is the New New York! Yeahhh baby! — Chris Harris

Portland, love the music and art scene much better than NYC!
R

Thank you for last night Portland. It was magical. You have the prettiest eyes! xox

See you next summer... hopefully!

Our Portland Story

A story project founded by Melissa Delzio.
Edited by Sarah Koch.

©2010 Our Portland Story LLC
All rights reserved.
www.ourportlandstory.com
Melissa@OurPortlandStory.com

Featuring stories by:

Chris Alan……………………………57	Dan Haneckow …………………46	Elizabeth Perlas………………………67
Julie Almquist …………………… 44	Elizabeth Harrington ……………14	Kevin Perlas ……………………………43
Scott Ballard……………………………39	April Hauck ………………………52	Dan Peski ………………………………56
Rachel Beckman …………………42	Aimee Heigold……………………68	Steve Potestio …………………………49
Laura Sue Bentz	Mike Houck ………………………16	Michelle Ramin ………………………26
& Ben Garland……………75	Bryan Hoybook …………………51	Alex Rauch ……………………………37
J.C. Bingham …………………………8	Kerri Jones ………………………62	Francie Royce …………………………45
Simon Black……………………………28	Jodi Kansagor……………………58	Michael Royce ………………………47
Tiffany Lee Brown …………………77	Katy Kavanaugh …………………22	Ryan Scheel……………………………23
Emma Burke …………………………73	Amber J. Keyser, Ph.D. …………29	Jennifer Sherowski …………………66
Walker Cahall…………………………20	Chris Kruell ………………………64	Steve Snell ……………………………81
Joy Cartier ……………………………63	Scott Latham ……………………50	Paul Sorenson…………………………19
Joanna Ceciliani………………………15	Luis Ponce de Leon ……………71	Suzy Vitello Soulé ……………………76
Jenny Cestnik…………………………78	Lois Leveen ………………………24	Kim Stafford …………………………40
Scott Cushman ………………………32	Hilary Lowenberg………………54	Kristin Thiel & Ali McCart…………41
Eloise Damrosch ……………………60	Janet Lunde ………………………79	Alissa & Justin Thiele………………36
Steve Gronert Ellerhoff ……………48	Ronald Stewart Marshall………38	Roberta Tsuboi………………………30
Natalie Morad El-Jourbagy …………6	Sue Marshall………………………82	June O. Underwood…………………61
Miriam Feder …………………………11	Richard Mavis……………………69	Jeffery Van Vleck……………………33
Byron Ferris …………………………13	Molly McClurg	C.J. White ……………………………53
Colleen Flory…………………………65	& Tory Van Wey …………27	Matt J. Wiater…………………………70
Ariel Frager …………………………34	David Metzger……………………72	Brian T. Wilson ………………………12
Alice Francis …………………………17	Dustin Micheletti…………………35	Molly Wolverton & Tal Caspi……18
Janet Freeman ………………………55	Merrick Monroe…………………25	Yuvi Zalkow……………………………80
Vincent Green ………………………21	Patsy Moreland ……………………7	Carole Zoom …………………………74
Rebecca Gregor………………………31	Michael Munk……………………10	
Alice Gustafson…………………………9	Lisa Parsons………………………59	

Welcome

On the following pages you will experience the results of a project affectionately dubbed *Our Portland Story*. This project paired stories about Portland, written by locals describing one thing they love about their city, with designers who brought their stories visually to life on the page.

As a Portlander of six years, I thought I was fairly well-versed in the many likable attributes of our city. I made assumptions as to the type of stories I was going to receive after posting an open call for submissions for this book. I figured all the typical guidebook hot spots would get equal and adequate coverage. Instead, the submissions I received surprised me in their broad scope, unique voice, and focus on details of our city that were far from the obvious. In addition, the historical perspective that some authors gave to the book elevated the quality, and added a deeper level of connection and meaning to the place I call home.

This book, for me, has been an incredible learning experience. I have started a running list of "places to explore" in Portland, springing from my reading of the submissions, bolstered by my subsequent research on their background. This process renewed my own love for this city. There are always new places — natural and manmade — to explore and discover. And if you tire of the new, you can always review history and rediscover the old.

~Melissa Delzio, founder of Our Portland Story

The Book

Our Portland Story Volume One is the work of 77 authors, 68 designers, one editor and one founder. The stories were collected from local Portlanders following an open call for submissions in September of 2008. It took over a year to edit those stories, pair each story with a designer, and work with the designer and author to create the resulting page. Each page in the book represents a different story told by a different author and designed by a different designer.

Additionally, on page 83 you will find Story Notes, a section where specific background information and details related to the story are given for each entry in the book.

This book is by no means a complete look at the City of Portland. Rather, it represents insights by 77 different people. Many locals reading this book may be shocked to see that their favorite places/things/events/people are not mentioned. That is why this book is an ongoing, live, evolving project. Our Portland Story is already seeking story submissions for the next book, *Our Portland Story Volume Two*, which is planned for release in 2012.

The project will continue to produce books on a two-year cycle, so long as the community enjoys and supports the output. Additionally, the website, www.ourportlandstory.com, will house all the stories from each book as it is released. Please visit the website to add your voice to the project and submit your story to the next volume of the book. Thank you, and keep making Portland a beautiful place to live.

Artwork to left, by artist Michelle Ramin titled, **SE Alder and 44th**

I wake up every day and the first thing I do is gaze out of my window to see what the sky has in store for me.

In that moment I am reminded, once again, of how lucky I am to live in downtown Portland, Oregon. I love how the water tower and "Made in Oregon" sign shimmer in the distance, protecting the city from the east.

Every day I see both icons as they were the day before, yet every day what changes is the beautiful sky. Not only does the sky change daily, but the sign itself has changed twice, starting out as "White Satin," for the White Satin Sugar Company, then becoming "White Stag" in 1957. It was only in 1996 that it changed to what we see today, "Made in Oregon."

Will It Change Again?

A couple of months after submitting the above to Our Portland Story, I got word that the sign is indeed undergoing another facelift. The University of Oregon purchased the sign, but instead of it reading "University of Oregon," they compromised with the City of Portland to change it to just read "Oregon." What do I think about it all? I'm used to change and am happy with it saying "Oregon" because, after living here now for almost four years, I feel like an Oregonian, though I wasn't born (made) in Oregon. The sign now will have even more meaning for me.

By Natalie El-Jourbagy :: www.portnatalia.blogspot.com

I am a native of PORTLAND, OR.

I have lived in other places in the United States, but Portland brings me back to the place of my 1939 birth, chosen by my emigrating ancestors who passed their love for the area onto their children. As I look back upon my childhood, I think of what I miss, centering around **family**, **food**, **music**, **exercise**. These themes are still in my life today, but I would now add **art**. I didn't think, when I was younger, about how much my parents worked at giving us a great foundation for our future lives. We weren't rich, but my parents knew how to enrich our lives with things to **see** and **do**.

I miss:

...going to **Jantzen Beach** for swimming lessons with Tye Steinbach as the instructor in the summer.

...occasional visits to the **Tik Tok Drive-in** on Sandy Blvd, where the servers delivered the food to your car and wore roller skates.

...going to **Yaw's Restaurant**, in the Hollywood District, for hamburgers and shakes.

...Saturday afternoon movies at the theater on **Alberta Street**.

...**Raven Dairy** where I would go with my grandmother so she could have fresh buttermilk and I could watch the donut machine.

...walking over the squares of glass in the sidewalks **downtown**.

...the **Vernon Ice Cream store**, in NE Portland, for the best ice cream.

...roller skating at **Oaks Park** and at another rink above Union Avenue, down near the Morrison Bridge.

...taking the **downtown trolley** to the **library**.

...boating with our parents on the **Columbia River**.

...**watching the shoemaker** making wooden shoes near the Multnomah Hotel on my way to a **cello lesson**.

story by: PATSY MORELAND *illustration by:* SEAN GARRISON

WRITTEN BY:
J.C. BINGHAM

DESIGNED BY:
ADAM SIRKIN

Portlanders can thank their own enlightened cussedness for revealing and keeping the city's treasures in its neighborhoods. Yes, neighborhoods, where discovery is a best friend. It's what helped me and my wife fall in love all over again.

We were married toward the end of 1988 in a church under the Fremont Bridge. We were soon parents, buying a home and letting work and the domestic machine click along. Time passed, settling and lulling us into believing that routine meant stability. In the years our daughter went from Barney the Dinosaur to Borrowing the Car, a certain fearlessness in our affection began to ebb more than flow. The sensation was not unlike a made-for-TV-movie: we'd lost something, and we needed a way to reclaim it.

cuss·ed (ksd)
adj. Informal
1. Perverse; stubborn.
2. Cursed.

It took a little extra in the way of pillow talk, raised voices and silent tears, but we eventually arrived at a bilateral awesome idea: The Standing Saturday Coffee Date. As rain fell (because it was March), we committed to stumble on a new spot every Saturday morning. Large chains that use words like star and bucks in their signage were nonstarters. And as long as we were going to be sitting across from each other (or side-by-side if sinking into a secondhand sofa), we'd see if we could not talk about our daughter.

INTRA MARITAL AFFAIR

With so many walks and coffeehouses and bakeries and brewpubs in this city — and people who cross and connect by a lot less than six degrees — we soon felt like adulterers, indulging in an affair with Portland and ourselves. For the last four years, we've rolled out of bed to find new favorites in Kenton, Sellwood, Arbor Lodge, Lair Hill, Beaumont, St. Johns, Goose Hollow, Buckman, Ladds, Multnomah, and more. Thank you, Portland. Over Americanos or triple lattes, we'd inhale warm muffins and absorb the sidewalk ethos in all its weekend glory. We'd revel in the moment, notice things. Imagine that.

We found each locally owned retreat to be a locus of sorts — revealing a big strand of DNA with its own twisting colors and building blocks that make Portland Portland. And through all that discovery — our deep gratitude to talented baristas everywhere — a magical transference occurred. We not only re-fell in love with our city and each other, but I also rediscovered my best friend.

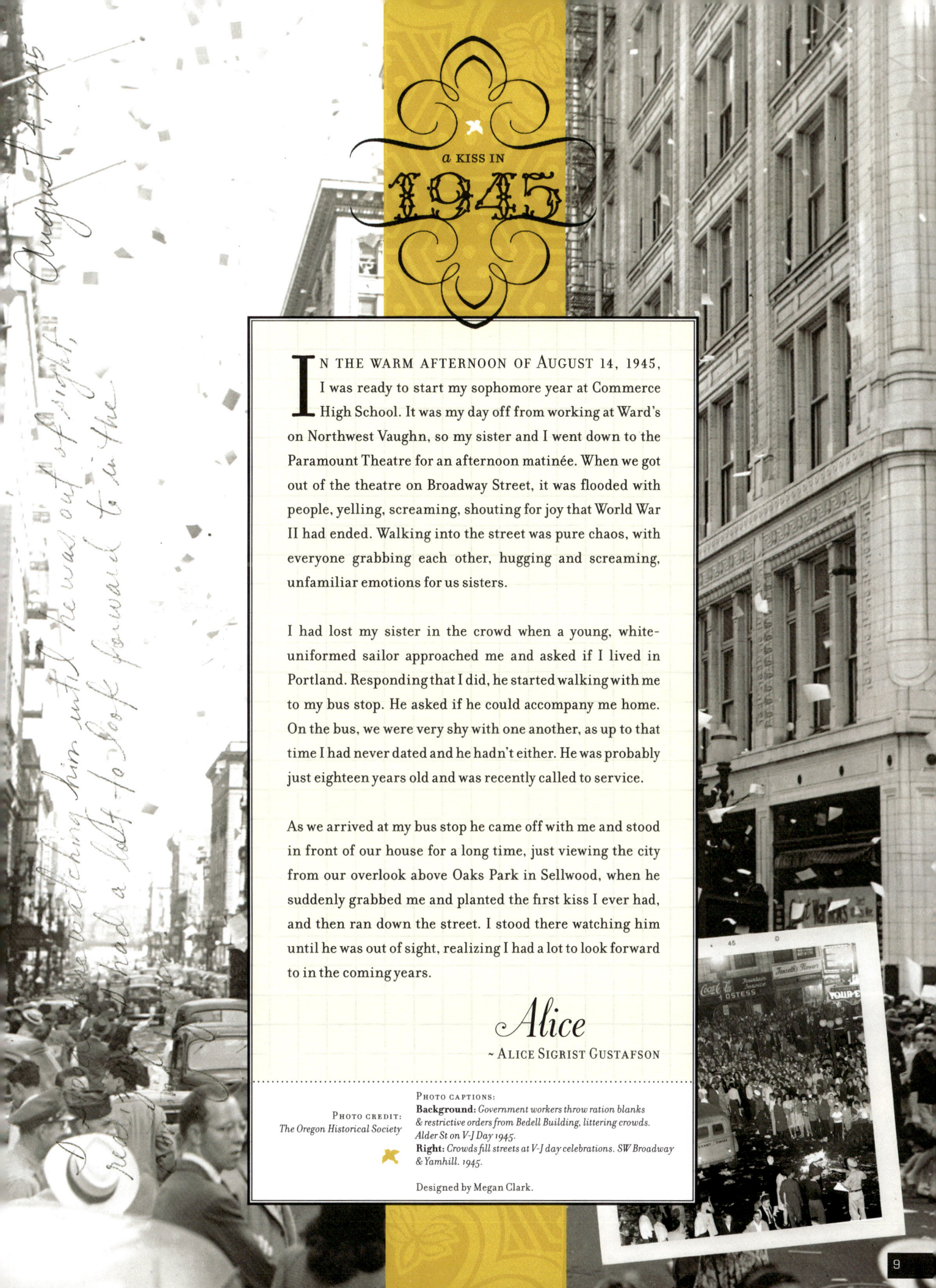

A KISS IN 1945

IN THE WARM AFTERNOON OF AUGUST 14, 1945, I was ready to start my sophomore year at Commerce High School. It was my day off from working at Ward's on Northwest Vaughn, so my sister and I went down to the Paramount Theatre for an afternoon matinée. When we got out of the theatre on Broadway Street, it was flooded with people, yelling, screaming, shouting for joy that World War II had ended. Walking into the street was pure chaos, with everyone grabbing each other, hugging and screaming, unfamiliar emotions for us sisters.

I had lost my sister in the crowd when a young, white-uniformed sailor approached me and asked if I lived in Portland. Responding that I did, he started walking with me to my bus stop. He asked if he could accompany me home. On the bus, we were very shy with one another, as up to that time I had never dated and he hadn't either. He was probably just eighteen years old and was recently called to service.

As we arrived at my bus stop he came off with me and stood in front of our house for a long time, just viewing the city from our overlook above Oaks Park in Sellwood, when he suddenly grabbed me and planted the first kiss I ever had, and then ran down the street. I stood there watching him until he was out of sight, realizing I had a lot to look forward to in the coming years.

Alice
~ ALICE SIGRIST GUSTAFSON

PHOTO CREDIT:
The Oregon Historical Society

PHOTO CAPTIONS:
Background: *Government workers throw ration blanks & restrictive orders from Bedell Building, littering crowds. Alder St on V-J Day 1945.*
Right: *Crowds fill streets at V-J day celebrations. SW Broadway & Yamhill. 1945.*

Designed by Megan Clark.

Woody Guthrie,

WORLD-FAMOUS COMPOSER OF OUR NATIONAL FOLK ANTHEM "THIS LAND IS YOUR LAND," IS ONE OF THE FEW RADICALS OFFICIALLY HONORED IN PORTLAND. HOWEVER, HE IS NOT HONORED BY THE CITY OF PORTLAND, BUT RATHER STEALTHILY BY THE FEDERAL GOVERNMENT'S BONNEVILLE POWER ADMINISTRATION (BPA).

In 2001, with almost no publicity, the administration named the driveway at its headquarters "Woody Guthrie Circle," and erected three stones inscribed with verses from two of his 26 songs inspired by the Columbia River, "Roll on Columbia" and "Pastures of Plenty." A large tapestry of Guthrie also hangs in the lobby of the BPA building at 905 NE 11th Avenue. Much of the credit for the memorial goes to two BPA employees: folk singer Bill Murlin and retired employee Elmer Buehler. It was Buehler who drove Guthrie around the Columbia River region in 1941, later rescuing some of his recordings that the government intended to discard.

Woody Guthrie substation at Odell.

In contrast, a year before the 2001 dedication, Guthrie's name was removed from the BPA's substation in Hood River when ownership was transferred to the Hood River Electric Co-op. Hood River's anti-Communist business leaders, who also removed Japanese-American names from the town's honor roll during World War II, objected to the original designation in 1990.

In 2000, they pressured the Co-op board to rename it for Willard Johnson, its first manager. They acted with unintentional irony, having forgotten that Johnson himself had strongly supported the Guthrie name against the local opposition, declaring that the "world would be better off with a few more Woody Guthries in it."

Written by Michael Munk, www.michaelmunk.com
Design by Marisa D. Green, Studio Danae.

Illustration from Tribute to Woody Guthrie, Store Front Theater, 1967.

When all my assumptions broke into pieces—
sharp, slithery, and none-too-shiny—
Portland spoke through my ticklish in-step.
She pressed into the soles of my feet with
rose-and-tumble acceptance,
as I skirted puddles known and unknown.

Restless possibility swayed along my sides
while Portland steadied my stride—"It's ok."
Who knew that asphalt could be a tender touch?
That this patient, old-friend town of mine
would roll out padding and take me easy,
while the stuffing in my head blew 'round.

poem by Miriam Feder
illustration by Jacqueline Bos

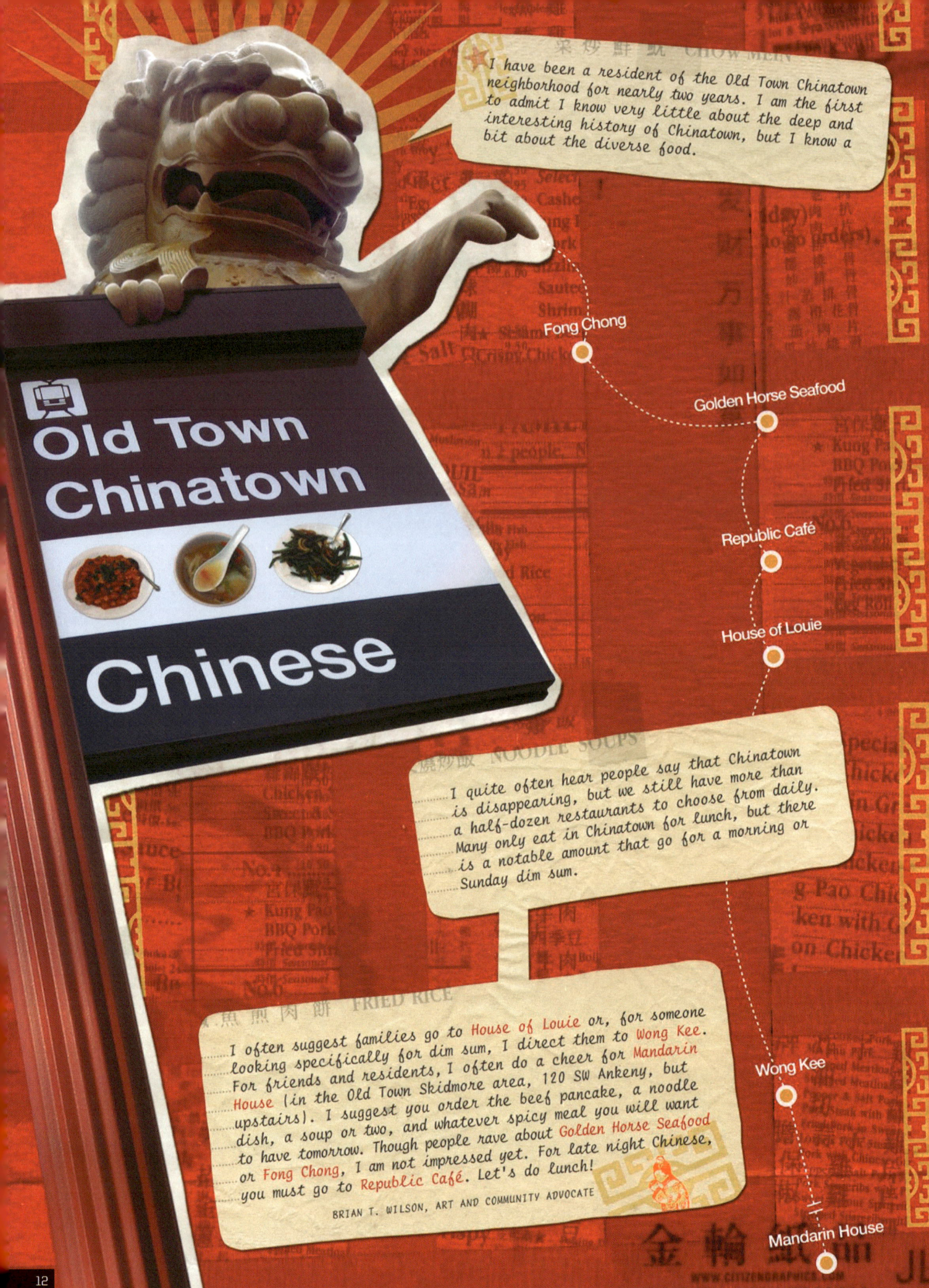

I have been a resident of the Old Town Chinatown neighborhood for nearly two years. I am the first to admit I know very little about the deep and interesting history of Chinatown, but I know a bit about the diverse food.

I quite often hear people say that Chinatown is disappearing, but we still have more than a half-dozen restaurants to choose from daily. Many only eat in Chinatown for lunch, but there is a notable amount that go for a morning or Sunday dim sum.

I often suggest families go to House of Louie or, for someone looking specifically for dim sum, I direct them to Wong Kee. For friends and residents, I often do a cheer for Mandarin House (in the Old Town Skidmore area, 120 SW Ankeny, but upstairs). I suggest you order the beef pancake, a noodle dish, a soup or two, and whatever spicy meal you will want to have tomorrow. Though people rave about Golden Horse Seafood or Fong Chong, I am not impressed yet. For late night Chinese, you must go to Republic Café. Let's do lunch!

BRIAN T. WILSON, ART AND COMMUNITY ADVOCATE

portland's creative HOMER

BY BYRON FERRIS
DESIGNED BY: CRE8TIVEGIRL

In 1952, Portland's second television channel came to town bringing network TV to a market area that was approaching one million. The new channel announced a contest to the advertising creatives of the nation, a contest to do an ad that would put KGW on the marketing map. Back then, the standard way to create an ad was to picture the product and write "5 Reasons Why" the reader should buy it. Portland's Homer Groening, a recent graduate from Linfield College, was working in Portland at an ad agency as a copywriter. Homer entered the contest with the ad shown here. Homer's ad broke the rules. Not only did it show a nekked woman, but it expressed a negative in the headline.

Homer's ad won the local contest and then won again, nationally, selected by a panel of ad luminaries. The prize was a Hillman auto, large enough for the Groening family, including Homer, Margaret, and the kids, Maggie, Lisa, and Matt. Homer soon opened up his own ad agency, Homer Groening Advertising, and within a month had a major client, the Jantzen International Sports Club. Many other career successes followed for Homer, including pro photoshoots in Hawaii, promotions for the Benson and Portland's Pioneer Courthouse Square, and, later, movie-making.

'YOU AND YOUR DAMN TOTAL TELEVISION
I get up in the morning, plug in the coffeemaker. On my way to the shower I turn on the set. And you know very well what happens. You are in cahoots with NBC. You show overwhelming shows. You use the most electricity. The best news, the best special events, the best everything. In color. Even the other stations in Portland tune in; they might as well, everyone else does. It's all fine and good for you and your advertisers to stand there self-satisfied and smirking. But what can I tell my husband when he gets home? Here he comes now, up the driveway. Shall I tell him I watch KGW-TV all day? Hello, honey. I said, hello, honey. Oh well. There's no problem. He's just standing here by my side, watching. This is
TOTAL TELEVISION, **KGW-TV**, PORTLAND you know.'

PERHAPS SEEING HIS DAD SUCCEED IN THIS CREATIVE BUSINESS PROMPTED HOMER'S SON, MATT GROENING, TO CREATE "THE SIMPSONS," TELEVISION'S LONGEST RUNNING TV CARTOON SHOW. HE USED THE FAMILY'S NAMES WITH "BART" BEING AN ANAGRAM OF "BRAT." BUT HOMER GROENING WAS NEVER THE OAFISH HOMER SIMPSON. HE WOULD NEVER HAVE SAID "DOH!" IN HIS CREATIVE LIFE.

The Wishing Well
BAR AND RESTAURANT

St. Johns was a town that became part of Portland in 1915. Tourist information and neighborhood guides always mention that it still has a small-town feel. Maybe that's why I like it; I moved to Portland from a small Midwestern town. St. Johns is decidedly un-hip, which is another reason I like it.

I also like dive bars, and St. Johns has its share. The Wishing Well, where they advertise "Chinese and American Food," is one of them.

Libby Harrington
typesetter

Designed by Veronika Buck Valentova
Photos by Dan4th, Ceanandjen

I love Portland because
it sings to me!

by Joanna Ceciliani

I wanted to perform from as far back as I can remember. I used to stand in front of one of our windows and ask one of my brothers or my sister to pull the shade up and down so I could pretend to be a singer being introduced on stage.

Influences have so much to do with our makeup and I believe it all started when my father built, and my mother handled the business side of, a dance hall called Division Street Corral (later known as D-Street). It opened in December of 1948 and was an immediate success, featuring all types of western artists including Hank Thompson, Merle Travis, Ray Price and Johnny Cash. When rock and roll hit the music scene, my parents were forced to bring in acts like Bobby Darin, Roy Orbison, The Knickerbockers, Paul Revere and the Raiders, Bobby Vee, and Bobby Vinton.

At the age of 18, I was signed on to a group called the New Oregon Singers and ended up traveling the world. I was also part of a quartet that was styled after a group called the Manhattan Transfer. And later, after many personal changes, I chose to answer an ad in the Oregonian for opera singers. I didn't know what an aria was at the time but auditioned with "Raindrops on Roses" and made it into the Portland Opera Chorus for two shows, unpaid. I continued to study voice and sang for the next 21 years and have just now retired. I don't know what is next for me but in this city, I feel anything is possible! I don't believe it could have happened in any other city. It has always been a musical town.

Opening Night - Dec. 1948

Adeline and Charley Ceciliani (Corral's 10th Anniversary)

design : Jay Cech

Standing on the bluff overlooking **Oaks Bottom Wildlife Refuge,** one can look to the north where lies an expanse of wetlands, riparian, and open water habitat, framed by big-leaf maples and black cottonwoods. Ross Island sits in the near distance, Portland's downtown skyline in the middle distance, and steam can be seen rising from Mount St. Helens in the far distance.

On recent nature walks around the 160-acre wetland, I've seen five **bald eagles** perched in one tree off SE Sellwood Boulevard; another three young eagles playing follow-the-leader through the nearby trees; **red-tailed hawks** engaged in circus-like aerobatics with **osprey** ferrying still-wriggling carp back to their nest on East Island; **peregrine falcons** staffing a family of **Anna's hummingbirds** in the parking lot at Sellwood Park; and a family of **river otter** playing in the mud. I've seen over fifty **great blue herons** standing thigh high in the wetlands, while flocks of **green-winged teal, American wigeon, ring-necked ducks, common mergansers**, and **coots** glide past.

Portland has a wealth of wildlife, spectacular views, and places for quiet contemplation, all literally in the heart of the city. The best part, though, is that there are large and small **nature oases** and **ribbons of green lining streams** and **rivers** throughout the Portland-Vancouver region. While other regions may boast a wealth of urban greenspaces, none can lay claim to the wonderful juxtaposition of urban nature nearby and fabulous rural landscape. Within a mere fifteen to twenty minutes of my NW Portland apartment, I can be **kayaking** on the Willamette, Columbia, or Columbia Slough; **riding** my bike or **walking** along the Springwater Trail or through a 5,000-acre forested park; **birding** intensely urban Oaks Bottom or serenely rural Sauvie Island.

Similarly, after my outing I can, once again within a few-minutes' **walk**, repair to any number of brewpubs for a Blue Heron ale, Hammerhead ale, or Lucky Lab stout or to one of a host of great restaurants.

— *Mike Houck*
www.urbangreenspaces.org

The CAST-IRON HERITAGE of PORTLAND

By Alice Francis
Design by Raymond G. Perez

In the mid 19th century, cast-iron was developed as a building material. The great cities of Europe and the Eastern United States had already been built, for the most part. It was at this time, however, that Portland was developing as a city. Some of the rarest architecture in the world developed in our city during the latter part of the 1800s.

The founding fathers of Portland invested in the city by building fabulous cast-iron structures in the period's popular Italianate style. They used cast-iron for structural pieces and decorative embellishment for the building facades that were pre-fabricated in foundries and assembled at the building site.

The architectural heritage that our city's founding fathers left behind has been grossly under-appreciated. We once boasted 180 such structures but, during the 20th century, most had undergone demolition leaving around 20 at present. Even so, Portland has the second largest collection of cast-iron buildings, second only to New York City's Soho District.

A trip to Portland's Skidmore/Old Town neighborhood reveals a glimpse of what once was. Although most of our cast-iron buildings are gone, many replaced by parking lots, one can imagine how stunning the sight must have been, the continuous, unbroken repetition of line, carving out arches and columns in building after building. The handsome Italianate facades, each one original in its own way, contributed to a unified civic design in Portland's early history.

What is left of our cast-iron heritage is by no means safe from further destruction, but efforts to restore Old Town are being considered. Salvaged cast-iron columns, arches, and various embellishments are in storage waiting to be used in proposed projects. There are rare and wonderful opportunities to restore Portland's cast-iron heritage in Skidmore/Old Town. What is needed is creativity, along with a healthy dose of imagination, followed by commitment. ⚜

Sources: Hawkins, William John. *Portland's Historic New Market Theatre.* Copyright 1983 Portland, Published by William John Hawkins, III

Hawkins, William John. *The Grand Era of Cast-Iron Architecture in Portland.* Binford & Mort/Portland. Copyright 1976

Lower Photo by Raymond G. Perez

On October 27, 2008, Portland was for a time overrun with the undead. More precisely, downtown Portland was swarmed by a ZOMBIE PARADE.

It was one of several cities in the U.S. whose zombie population came out in flesh-peeling glory that day, but to me, Portland's citizens gave it a flavor far apart from any old brain-feasting party.

Portland's zombies were a reflection of the city they love:

BIZARRE ORIGINAL AND COMFORTABLY SELF-CONSCIOUS

I encountered the zombie parade and found that every participant was so immersed in their role as an animated corpse that I began to believe they were real. I couldn't take pictures of the glazed eyes, rotting flesh, and tattered clothing without thinking I was somehow in the middle of a Bruce Campbell film.

And that's where imagination and incredible gory makeup intersected...

By Molly Wolverton
Photos by Tal Caspi

THE FACE:
I can't describe it, you have to see for yourself. I wanted to reach out and pop one of those pustules bubbling on her face. See if it oozed clear or purple and green. Her eyes shone out from within the sea of scarred flesh and she groaned. I got her picture right before she charged at me, causing the other zombie parade participants to circle in on me like they were seagulls and I was a piece of bread. I barely escaped that one.

Designed by Joe Aimonetti

By Paul Sorenson
Photo by Charles Young
Design by Kat Topaz

I first came upon one of the horse rings outside the Nob Hill Grill on NW 23rd Ave., where some VERY large cast-metal hogs were chained to one of these iron rings bolted into the curb.

I thought it was a lot of work, but a good idea, to keep the statues safe from metal-snatchers. But then I began noticing the rings in other locations, on other streets and, occasionally, they had a small, plastic horse tethered to them.

Back in the 1800s, horses were the main mode of transportation. Across Portland, iron "horse rings" were embedded into the curbstones that were laid as late as the 1920s. They have remained there since, and not until 2005 did they garner more than rain and leaves and the odd glance (and a trip or two, I'd bet).

In 2005, artist Scott Wayne Indiana started the Horse Project when he tied his first small plastic pony to a horse ring in northwest Portland. For a few months he continued parking the ponies at rings all over town, and then he started asking the public to join in. One enthusiast claims to have tethered upwards of 150 miniature mounts all over Portland.

The idea seems so idiosyncratic and a bit "odd," but endearingly so. It has that sense of sly playfulness and quiet "I do it because it makes me smile" that—to me—typifies Portland. We don't mind doing things folks in the midwest would find downright weird—we revel in it.

These memories stick out like crystal clear gems in my sometimes-foggy existence.

Portland Memories

These are rich remembrances instead of the haphazard cognitions that I usually have. They are extremely vivid and triggered by the sights and sounds of puddle city. These memories are quick vignettes from my first months in Portland, a time where everything was new to me. The ideas would form suddenly and ingrain themselves instantly in my consciousness. I came to define these quick pulses of information as Portland **Memories.**

Whether the memory is walking over the Steel Bridge on a drizzly winter day watching the last vestiges of the sun sink beneath the West Hills, or talking to a drunk man who may or may not have had a gun in his pocket, or bringing my girlfriend home on the handlebars of my trusty bicycle, these memories are crystal clear gems, contrasting with my sometimes-foggy **Existence.**

The more Portland Memories I make, though, the more vague they become. The stuff of these specific memories now comprises my normal daily interactions. These wonderfully crafted snippets have become my existence. Everyday is filled with a thrilling adventure, a comical interaction, or a breathtaking vista of downtown Portland. Some would call this mundane, but I for one think it is **Amazing.**

"There's something about the BRIDGES," she said.

_Yes, the bridges, and in particular for me, that beautiful black behemoth, the Steel. Im not sure what I love about this bridge. Its closeness to the river it crosses, its industrial architecture, its seemingly massive presence. Perhaps, because to walk it is to know it. I've crossed its lower deck many times but one dark, quiet night stands out. 2 am. The Willamette is still. Cold and thick. Black as coffee. So close it could reach out and touch me and take me to the depths forever. Reality Check. Im on the Steel Bridge and quite safe. I walk on slowly, so as to savor the magic of this night. Halfway across and a powerful freight engine crawls onto the bridge from the eastside industrial yards, its headlamp a bright beacon in the blackness that surrounds me. As it creeps on past I can sense every machination of its forward movement, hear the muted crescendo of steel on steel as it pulls a rhythmic parade behind it. It belongs here and the Steel comes alive with the rumble of its presence. Now the train sounds from the westside city and, wishing only to stay and know more, I walk on, knowing that I'll be back to experience this bridge and everything that is a part of it.

The river, the trains, and Portland

Vincent Green, Gardener/author
Gerry Blakney, Designer

Yeah, there is something about the bridges.

21

THE EDGE OF PORTLAND

by Katy Kavanaugh

illustration by Freshbeast

I cannot write a Portland paean as yet, due to my deep sand- and fog-soaked roots. I'm encouraged, though, by the all-weather cyclists and the civic-mindedness of progressive Portlanders. Although there is that nourishment an artist draws from the pavement where she took her first steps, I've pledged to be a liaison between the two cities, Portland and San Francisco, as I ease my way into my future in one or the other. Even so, I have declared, very politely or under my breath, that Portland lacks the edge that I need from a city. But a few weeks ago, I found the edge while riding the Tri-Met #75, and felt relief… maybe even a little love.

Having been passed over a third time for a standby flight to San Francisco, I left the airport, taking the light rail for the first time back into town. There I transferred to the #75 bus at the Hollywood terminal. Travel frustrations combined with cold, wet weather had drained my patience. Finally, a break: there was a bus seat for me, further subduing certain words only recently allowed in my vocabulary.

I had stepped onto Noah's ark, it seemed. At least two of every Portland character was there. There were fifteen-year-old punks with ten-inch spiked Mohawks, dressed in fine torn black everything and, well, more spikes. There was the throng of loud, guileless teenage girls, scary to some, but delightfully inquisitive about the do-ing of the Mohawk style as they passed the boys. A squeaky clean family of four had to take separate seats. Dad was wearing a "Teachers for Obama" shirt and was reading to his son on one bench toward the back, while mom and daughter chatted about their mutual adoration of dried mango with a jovial woman who'd just returned from shopping at Trader Joe's and who was sharing her snacks with the front rows.

I was seated in the middle of the bus beside another rider who may have also taken the seat for its good view. He was calm, folded easily into the seat, watching it all with wonder, as I was.

To my right was a girl with a soft sculpture puppet she'd designed and a new admirer beside her. As they chatted, she animated the puppet as if it were participating in the conversation. Wow, puppets to the right with moms, mango and Mohawks to the left—okay, I'm a little enamored. But in front of me was a hefty guy in reflector garb. He seethed as he heard the punks voice their pro-Obama political opinions, muttering to himself "I hate that…" with a sort of Yosemite Sam hrrrumph. Curmudgeonly compelling as he was, I was a little nervous that ol' Sam might just be that perfect candidate to go postal.

I thought to myself, "It's my first #75 ride and I'm shot, ahhhh, what luck." Fortunately, the bus was too crowded for him to brandish any weapons or scissors at the Mohawks like I know he was fantasizing. I know he was. I located my exit.

I got off the ark at Division to walk the rest of the way home. As I walked, I envisioned, in vivid detail, what might have happened following my departure, and all flavored by my freshly Portland-spiced imagination. Oftentimes, I imagine the worst just in case it happens. On the #75 that day, it was easy to imagine the worst, but, in the end, I'm sure it was the best of character that was revealed.

EVOLUTIONARY JASS BAND

SIDE A
You're asleep and Jazz is dead.

It's a nightmare of high society and bad standards. Gone are the days of smoky clubs with hot and heartfelt playing. In its place are "high class lifestyle" musical venues.

"Hey, let's go watch some jazz!"

Suit. Tie. Evening dress. $20 cover. Dinner. Drinks. Dessert. Not even one song recognizable to the audience. Just something to do on Tues. with the Mr. or Mrs.

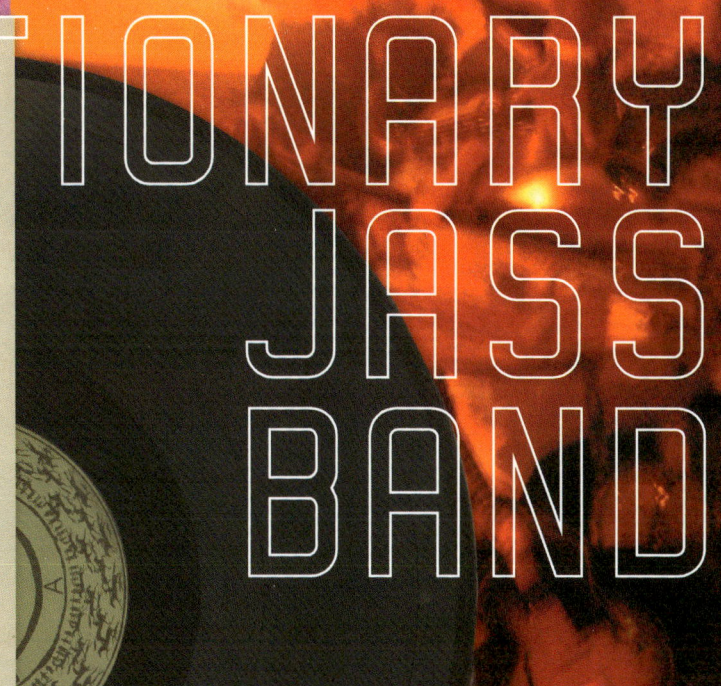

SIDE B
You are awake

now and the Evolutionary Jass Band is playing (though not on a stage, they don't do that). Jef Brown plays, occasionally lying on his back, conjuring up sounds that remind you of Trane, McLean, and Pharoah Sanders. Jesse Munro Johnson blows his lungs out running through the entire "cool" to "corner" circuit. Marisa and Michael ground everyone, whilst Bob takes off leading the band from classical to minimalist rock and back. Jazz is now alive because of EJB and every performance is what the two-bit suited hacks need to set their bar to. Grab your sneakers, leave your tie at home and go see them before you go back to sleep.

By Ryan Scheel

design by Melissa Delzio

One of the best things about Portland is the

Free Box

Maybe my affection for it stems from a reuse/recycle-oriented environmentalism. Or from an ethos of communal sharing. Or maybe just from my own cheapskate-itude. Whatever the reason, it's always a thrill: walking or biking through the city, you come upon a random cardboard box, the word FREE scrawled on the side in marker, and lean in to discover a seemingly arbitrary assortment of objects waiting to be claimed by passers-by. Clothing, cookbooks, a birthday gift for my snootiest neighbor—I've gotten it all out of a free box. And the old adage, "'Tis better to give than to receive" rings true regarding free boxes. Nothing is more entertaining than setting your discards out, then sneaking back inside to see what gets snatched up quickly and what lingers longest, as strangers pore over your stuff. But the true joy comes from the serendipitous reciprocity of both giving and receiving. Farewell, old camping cook-pots! Hello, hideous yet groovy candleholder! It's such a venerable Portland tradition that this past October, I saw someone ambling through the Last Thursday Alberta Art Walk, costumed for Halloween as a free box.

I happened upon this particular free box one bright June day. The donor's confusion of tambourines with cymbals pales next to the whimsical brilliance of using pot lids as percussion instruments. Perched downtown, the free box glimmered an unabashed invitation for someone to claim its bounty and make a RIGHTEOUS PORTLAND NOISE.

STORY & PHOTO BY LOIS LEVEEN
DESIGN BY DEANNA MICHAELSON

Everything about Portland is unique; walking downtown, I have never seen the same things nor had the same experience twice. I spotted this red vinyl pump on the corner of 2nd and Stark, just sitting on a newspaper dispenser. Who knows who put it there, or how long it sat untouched before some amused Portlander claimed it for themselves? How many people walked on by? It becomes hard not to appreciate all the unexpected beauty of this city... from the sunniest of days on the waterfront to most rainy nights in Chinatown, there is always some moment of remarkable truth to be seen. The beauty – and the story of Portland – is in the details, and the city wants you to see...

By Merrick Monroe / Design by Crystal Beasley

No one is from Portland.

a. Victoria Van Wey - Palo Alto, CA
b. Danielle Ventamiglia - Klamath Falls, OR
c. William Harlow - Chicago, IL
d. Michael Candelaria - San Jose, CA
e. Emily May - Burlington, VT
f. David Engler - Richmond, VA
g. Molly McClurg - Austin, TX
h. Kenneth Watson - Tallahassee, FL
i. Chernobyl - Los Angeles, CA

We all live together in Portland, but none of us is from Portland. We love the certain *je ne sais quoi* that pulled us to this city. It is this indefinable feeling that we are all here for, are committed to seeking out, and keeping alive.

Story and design by Molly McClurg

LONG SHADOWS

BY SIMON BLACK

These days I live in Portland. I came to Oregon once before, about four years ago. I'd been living in a small Canadian village for most of that year. We'd be up early each day, clambering for gear in the dark—hungover mostly—hardly uttering a word, so ingrained was the routine that any conversation would have been gratuitous. We'd snowboard all day—great long unending days—and we'd be talking non-stop about nothing but The Mountain.

Then one day The Mountain closed. I was tired and out of pocket, and the beat up old van we'd taken to Alaska was good for nothing now but scrap metal. We'd landed in Vancouver, BC, by default. It seemed a shame to end things there, where skyscrapers instead of mountains reached into the sky, and no deer or bear would be found. So, we hopped onto a Greyhound and headed south. Then, all of a sudden, Portland came into the frame and the sky was new. Cozy but energized, with a sea breeze and wet forest smell. The sun angled down gently, with just enough light to make everything seem fake somehow, and yet more real. Shadows so long I felt young again, like a child surrounded by big things.

Portland had been an entirely unplanned leg of our journey and our temporary visas were done—it seemed like—just as soon as they had begun. Before I knew it, I arrived back home in Sydney, Australia. It was as if the sun never really set in Portland, it just kind of rode the curve of the earth. The street lights flickering on before the day was done.

Then, years later, on a busy Tuesday, I was walking down a Sydney street, buses rattling past as I hugged the walls of China Town, when I felt my phone vibrate.

"Hello, Mr. Black! I'm calling from the Kentucky Consular Center..." the accent was strong and seemed put on "...you've won our Green Card Lottery, sir, and we haven't heard a word from you!" Buses pulled in and out, rushing past. "I'm sorry? The line's bad, there's a lot of noise here. I didn't catch where you're calling from?"

"You should have received a letter from us?"
"I wasn't sure if it was real."

Another bus roared past and then the line went dead.

Next came months of paperwork and medical exams and questioning, followed by goodbyes and itineraries and more paperwork, everything happening in fast motion. Like an ant, busily surviving, I was in miniature, running through a universe I could not see.

Now, back in America on an open-ended visa, it feels good to be back. Today, when I was at a Clinton Street cafe lost in a book, the sun rose and the dappled light crawled through an open window and onto the pages. I looked out of the shadows and into the street, and realized I was sitting on the other side of the world again.

"YES, SIR, THIS IS REAL! WELCOME TO THE UNITED STATES..."

DESIGNED BY WHITNEY PHU

author: amber j. keyser - amberkeyser.com

i have lived other places
 i have even loved other places but
each one, in some way made me feel... well...
OTHER shocking really that i spent seventeen
of my THIRTY-EIGHT years as a resident alien in far-
flung non-portland places!

take NEW MEXICO -
that desert sucked ME DRY.

on trips back home one glimpse of that verdant swath of PDX runway on descent & every cell sighed "ah water!"

in Georgia my liberal bent betrayed me at every turn.
"BREAST-FEEDING IN PUBLIC? YOU MUST BE JOKING!"

the greener fringe in WASHINGTON rejected me for conservative leanings and insufficient drug use

in Thailand the touchy-feely, granola-girl ME proved TOO loud TOO gawky, TOO conspicuous

JUST WAY TOO MUCH.

only Costa Rica
gave portland a run for its money in the
♡-of-place arena. BOTH have coffee, wild
& riotous forests, high literacy &
endangered turtles

but the portland edge is simple
the city looks at me —
 adventurer, parent, writer,
 biologist, chicken mama
 locavore, environmentalist —
    — and says "mine. you are mine."

maybe... just maybe...
    this city even loves me.

photo: seth isenberg   design: krista messer

I have lived in Portland for 60 years. When I was six years old, my class from Holladay Grade School went across the street to an empty lot. We sat there, bored to tears, watching these older ladies — I think they were members of the Lloyd family — all dressed up, digging a hole in the ground. They probably were not that old, but when you are six, everyone looks old. We were told they were "breaking ground" — not that we knew what that meant.

For the next four or five years, I watched this hole turn into a huge construction site. As time went on, I anticipated the finished product: the Lloyd Center Shopping Mall.

I still have fond memories of the fragrance of the mall. The smell of caramel apples from Morrow's Nut House, the smell of French fries and milk shakes from J.J. Newberry, and the best smell of all was the fresh popped popcorn at Woolworth's. It was an open-air mall, so when you came into the stores from the outdoors, it smelled wonderful!

To this day, every time I smell these fragrances, I think of my childhood.

— By Roberta Tsuboi

Perhaps it's because I originally hail from the desert, and am awestruck at the plethora of water in Portland. Or perhaps it's because I am amazed at the city's willingness to provide hours of FREE entertainment to the general public. But whatever it is... I love all of the fountains and water features in this town! From the Salmon Street Springs Fountain at the Tom McCall Waterfront Park to the multiple wading pools in many of the city parks, this city is sure to keep you cool and entertained throughout those glorious summer months! Thanks, Portland.

Rebecca Gregor

Designed by Nonnie Wong

DOTS CAFE

DOTS CAFE is like the younger, rebellious sibling in Portland's affluent restaurant family. Its low profile entrance, dim lighting, and black velvet art decor are the culinary equivalent of the middle finger to hoity-toity dinner places. With its cash-only policy and half-vegan menu, it doesn't even care what other people think. It unapologetically serves up gratifying comfort food and looks cool doing it.

text by Scott Cushman / photos by Matt Vestal (Dots Cafe exterior view) & Jessie May Li (fries, lights & sign) / page design by Jessie May Li

Portland's BIG fish in a small sea

Story by Ariel Frager
Design by Ryan Schroeder

It was the late 1980s and Portland still had that gritty feeling, before they scrubbed the artist lofts and drug users clean from Downtown and called it the Pearl District. I used to feel like I needed a shower after extended trips to the city center, the air of Podunk regionalism clinging to my clothes. But not this night. It was a clear cold winter evening, the wet streets glistening reflected light from the surrounding buildings. My friend Seth and I had left a late night showing of some art film at the Guild Theatre and as we crossed the near-empty parking lot, we noticed a man standing outside in the crisp night with a movie camera pointed at the stunning Jackson Building Clock Tower.

"What are you doing," I naively asked.

"Shooting pick up shots for Gus Van Sant's new movie, *My Own Private Idaho*."

Starstruck, Seth and I said in unison, "Wow! Gus Van Sant, we are big fans." And indeed we were, the previous year having waited for hours at one of Portland's art film venues, the Koin Center Theatre, to see his previous movie, *Drugstore Cowboy*.

Fumbling, Seth asked the cinematographer if we could someday meet Gus Van Sant, since we were such big fans.

"Sure," he said and knocked on the window of the dark car next to him. "Gus is right here."

Never leaving his place in the back seat, we chatted with Gus Van Sant for several minutes. "We would love it if you came up to Lewis and Clark, where we go to college, to talk to the film production program we started."

"Yeah, no problem," Gus said. "I'd be happy to. Give me a call, I'm in the book."

We raced back to school, flipped open the first phonebook we could find and sure enough, Gus Van Sant had a listed number.

A DAY OF OLDHAM

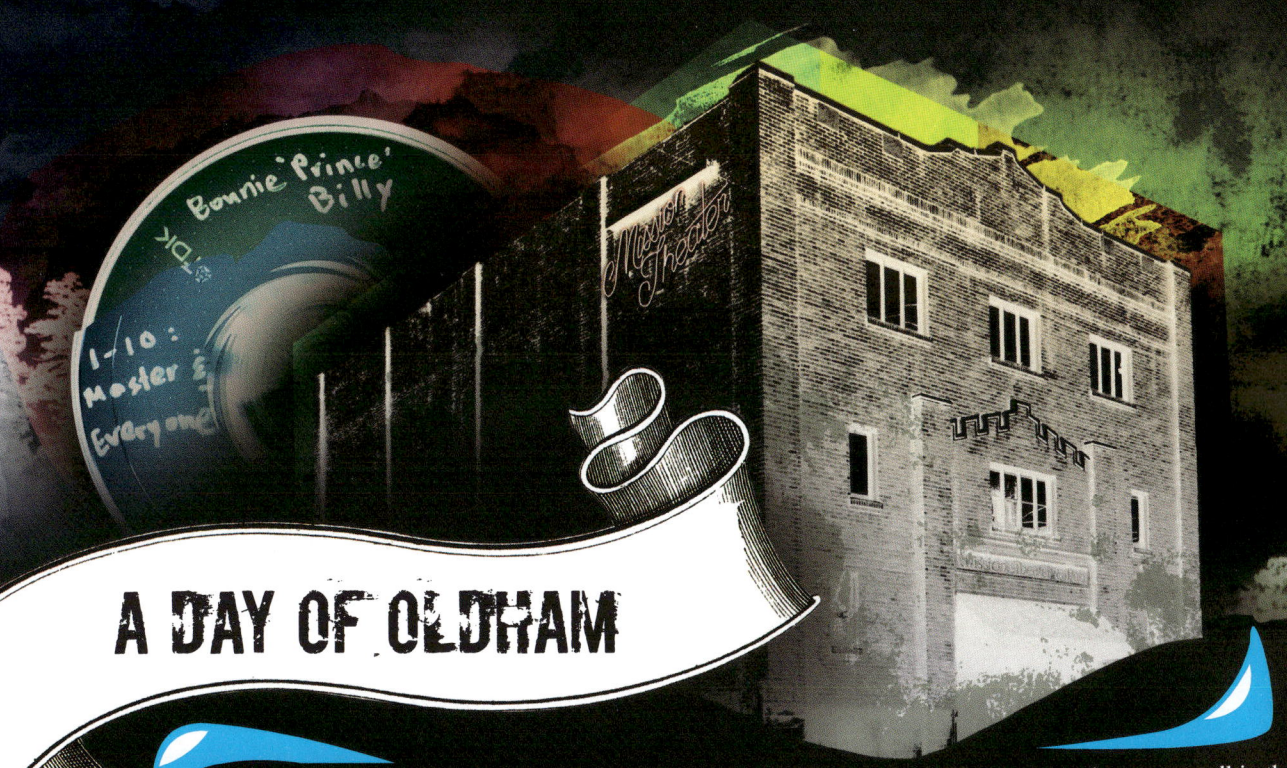

It was the first time I'd ever watched a film and then attended one of the main actor's music concerts, all in the same theater. The location was the Mission Theater, part of the McMenamin's empire, the movie was *Old Joy*, and the actor/musician was Will Oldham (AKA Palace Music AKA Palace Brothers AKA Bonnie "Prince" Billy).

Old Joy appealed to me for a couple of reasons. Not only am I an enormous fan of the "road film," but I especially like those dealing with issues of failing friendships, social awkwardness, and the stagnation of life and energy caused by increased responsibility. The soundtrack (courtesy of Yo La Tengo) perfectly accompanied the urban city and primeval rainforest settings. Much of the first half of the film was shot on location in Portland, tickling my more vainglorious side. Unfortunately, there were quite a few geographic inconsistencies during this Portland segment, e.g., crossing west over the Burnside Bridge and ending up in front of the Bagdad Theater on the east side of the Willamette River. A particularly memorable scene was an extended visit to the Bagby Hot Springs (located near Estacada along the western slopes of the Cascades), where Will Oldham's character utters this gem,

"SORROW IS NOTHING BUT WORN OUT JOY."

The concert followed the film a few hours later in the day, time passed easily at Powell's Books down the street. Human Bell opened up nicely, followed by Will Oldham and his mostly-extraneous band. He has a voice that is inhumanly tender, yet at the same time dangerously razor-edged, a rusty blade caressing softest skin, such intensity and depth of emotion, yet threatening to crumble into nothingness at each breath. "Worn out joy" would be an apt description of the man's lyrics, the words forcing a slight smile to play upon my lips as my heart filled with sadness. Will Oldham is hard to watch in person. He's constantly fidgeting, picking up scraps of paper, putting his hands in his pockets, tapping band mates on the shoulder, wiping his forehead with a hanky, cuffing his pant legs, adjusting his microphone, standing on one leg like a seagull, then crossing his legs and shivering like a preschooler holding his piss in. His body was pure chaos, but his voice always seemed to be aimed directly and solidly at the microphone, a disconcerting juxtaposition of sensory inputs that never failed to keep my attention. It was a wonderful show and, paired with the film, a great experience.

My thanks, Will.

by Dustin Micheletti

DESIGN AND THEATER PHOTO BY **ANDREW PETRIE**

Voodoo doughnut

One establishment that piqued our curiosity about Portland was Voodoo Doughnut. While we contemplated moving here from the rolling plains of Nebraska, we stumbled across their web site.

Voodoo Doughnut illustrated our idea of Portland...quirky, creative, and comfortable in its own skin. We learned that the founders didn't have any previous doughnut-making experience, but they weren't afraid to try something totally outside of their knowledge and trust their own creativity. Beyond creating quirky doughnuts like the Cap'n Crunch Berry and the Bacon Maple Bar, they perform legal weddings under a classy Isaac Hayes velvet painting. Keepin' Portland weird, FTW! Subsequently, after moving to Portland, Voodoo Doughnut was one of our first stops and it was everything we hoped it would be.

SAN DIMAS HIGH SCHOOL FOOTBALL RULES!

Justin & Alissa Thiele

page design, illustration and top photos by Brittany Hanson

First Thursday is over. I continue to feel a lingering, fresh buzz from seeing the vibrant multiplicity of new shows. As a result, my eye seems sharper than normal, and my mind, more aware. I gain inspiration from those works that incited my wonderment and receive courage from the kitsch, the groundbreaking, and all the art in between.

Each First Thursday is the day that heals the wrongs of the previous month. Its fresh extrospection shows us that contemporary art should have high hopes and high standards. My curiosity grows, anticipating the historical perspective of what I have witnessed. What, I eagerly ask, will decide the canon of the now in the future?

By Alex Rauch

designed by Alice Baldwin

Portlandia

by Ronald Stewart Marshall
photo by Sam Grover
design by Lisa Holmes/Yulan Studio

PORTLAND, OREGON, IS A **futuristic city that is an ever-growing, living art form in motion.** One symbol of the Rose City is the towering figure of the PORTLANDIA STATUE, SCULPTED BY ARTIST RAYMOND KASKEY. Her location is above the entrance of MICHAEL GRAVES' PORTLAND BUILDING in downtown Portland, at 1120 SW 5th Avenue. I see her as a mixture of different forms. She appears to be our own local version of THE STATUE OF LIBERTY, the SPIRIT OF BROOKLYN (the statue at the New York Public Library, Brooklyn), and the mythological KING NEPTUNE, all in one. With one of her bronzed and toned hands, **she reaches down to take us all along for the journey of discovery**; the journey that makes people everywhere long to come to Portland, the NEW MAGNET OF CREATIVITY. Her spear may be pointing downward to ward off any unsavory characters, like those insular, local people who want Portland to just stay back somewhere in the era of "Come to Oregon often, but don't move here," to paraphrase a quote from the late and great Oregon governor, Tom McCall. If he were here now, I'm sure he would change his point of view. Portland is "the city" to be in at this moment in time. **No longer is Portland just that nice green place where it rains.** PORTLAND IS A PLACE WHERE ANYTHING IS POSSIBLE AND ANYTHING GREAT MIGHT HAPPEN JUST BY BEING HERE AND BECOMING INVOLVED IN A MOMENT OF HER MAGIC.

Nestled

amidst

THE CAVALCADE OF STRESSFUL HOURS IN OUR LIVES ARE THE QUIET MOMENTS—THOSE RESTFUL TIMES WE CAN HANG OUR COATS ON AND EACH OF US IS ABLE TO DUB AS "MY **TIME**."

I'VE LIVED IN SEVERAL CITIES AND EACH HAS ITS OWN OFFERINGS IN WAYS TO SPEND THIS TIME. AS A SELF-PROFESSED BEER CONNOISSEUR IN TRAINING, I IMMEDIATELY NOTICED THE SHEER QUANTITY OF LOCAL BREWPUBS AND BREWERIES WHEN I MOVED TO PORTLAND. IT DIDN'T TAKE LONG BEFORE I NOTED SOMETHING UNIQUE SHARED AMONG THESE LOCAL HAUNTS—THEY OFFER A LOT MORE THAN WELL-CRAFTED BEER. THEY OFFER A SANCTUARY, A COMMUNITY LIVING ROOM WHERE FRIENDS AND STRANGERS CAN GATHER AND ENJOY THE SHARED EXPERIENCE OF BEING A **PORTLANDER.**

THIS YEAR HAS HAD ITS CHALLENGES AND NEXT YEAR WILL HAVE ITS OWN. THE THINGS WE CAN COUNT ON GROW FEWER ALL THE TIME, BUT IT DOESN'T HAVE TO BE THAT WAY. I AM REMINDED OF THIS WHEN I VISIT ONE OF MY **NEIGHBORHOOD** BREWPUBS. THERE ARE SOME PLACES WHERE TIME ALLOWS US TO RELAX AND ENJOY THE ANCIENT ART OF COMMUNITY—WHERE CONVERSATIONS IN THE COMPANY OF STRANGERS PREVAIL; NOT WORK, NOT HOME, BUT A NEUTRAL LANDSCAPE WHERE WE CAN ALL MEET ON **COMMON GROUND.**

FOR NOW, THIS MOMENT, SHARING A COLLECTIVE PINT IN A SMALL BREWPUB, NESTLED AMIDST THE CONVERSATIONS AND ELABORATIONS OF STRANGERS' TALES; THIS IS THE WAY IN WHICH I AM SPENDING THE BRIEF MOMENTS OF THIS EVENING'S "MY **TIME**."

BY SCOTT BALLARD (MYYEARINBEER.BLOGSPOT.COM) - DESIGN BY TWOGUITARS

HOW DO WE FIND OUR WAY IN PORTLAND?

BEGIN AGAIN PORTLAND

By Kim Stafford, writer

There are maps, street signs, helpful strangers—and for the wandering life, there is art. Portland makes public art part of the spirit-way-finding-fabric of the city. At the corner of SW 5th and Columbia—the intersection of two one-way streets—there is a blank façade of red granite begging for an image and a message. I wrote a little poem to put there for kin and strangers:

FRIEND, IT'S TIME TO TURN THE CORNER AND FIND WHERE YOU BEGAN.
BEGIN AGAIN WITH ALL YOU LOST BUT NEVER FORGOT.
REMEMBER WHEN YOU TASTED RAIN?
RISE UP WHERE ONE-WAY THINKING INTERSECTS SURPRISE.

The polished granite shows feathery compression patterns from the metamorphic forces that made the stone. So, along with the poem, we decided to cut into the stone images of Oregon sword ferns, those tough survivors of the old earth. Portland artist Anne Storrs gathered ferns, drew them obsessively, and printed the strongest images onto acetate to tape to the granite wall. Then she stood back to consider if they looked alive. Portland designer John Laursen took the words, sized them to fit the granite grid, then taped these words to the wall and stood back to consider. At last, the sandblaster has come to pummel the granite with garnet sand, and cut the words and ferns into this Portland wall for good. Deft graffiti.

Words and phrases drip from her mouth onto our eager ears. We absorb every ounce until the next author takes the mic, and a new shower of prose pitter-patters like the light rain tapping on the Convention Center roof... PORTLAND is a greenhouse of creativity and generosity, so we were wowed, but not shocked, when eleven teams of writers, and more than thirty local sponsors, joined Indigo Editing & Publications in a new approach to shattering writer's block, the **SLEDGEHAMMER** Writing Contest. Participants met at a northwest coffee shop—one pajama-clad man who had not heard about the contest happened in for a bagel and left on a mission of the imagination—and then took off on a scavenger hunt to Southwest, Southeast, and North Portland, collecting writing prompts and scrawling ideas in notebooks, of both the electronic and paper kinds. Thirty-six hours later eight stories, themselves seemingly breathless, their words bubbling off the page with adrenaline, had been submitted. The new Portland catchphrase: Sleep Is For Suckers. A Portlander who truly understands clocking writer's block,

Jan Underwood, the 2005 winner of the international 3-Day Novel Writing Contest, selected one **SLEDGEHAMMER** winner, and the two of them made one more stop on the Portland scavenger hunt: reading onstage at Wordstock.

—Ali McCart and Kristin Thiel, editors
Indigo Editing & Publications
(www.indigoediting.com)

My mom, Karen Steinbock, is the scooter babe of Southwest Portland. At first she's just a blur of pink in your rearview mirror, falling behind because her top speed is only 40 mph. But take a closer look and you'll see that she's riding a "Pink Hibiscus" Honda Metropolitan with a bubblegum-colored helmet to match. Sometimes she even wears hot pink shoelaces because she's a diva like that.

Mom bought her scooter last year in a fit of frustration over high gas prices. The Honda's one-gallon gas tank takes her 100 miles. She mostly rides it to Jazzercise, coffee shops and the grocery store. Beefy men on Harleys wave to her, which makes her feel like she's part of a "secret society" of two-wheelers (even if she's too nervous to let go of the handlebars to wave back). I live in Washington, D.C., now, but the last time I visited home, she taught me how to ride. I drove in wobbly, slow circles around our cul-de-sac, screaming and giggling the whole way.

If she thinks you don't see her, she'll give the cutest little "toot-toot" on her horn.

Watch out:

That's my mom on the road.

Story by Rachel Beckman, Journalist at The Washington Post / Design by Kris Travis

Dodge, Dip, Duck, Dive, and...Drink!

I signed up to play dodgeball in spring '05 expecting to play just one season, but 14 seasons later I'm hooked on the camaraderie, endless stream of new faces, and the opportunity to share brews with people I was pelting with a rubber ball a few minutes earlier.

I'm not alone in unleashing **my inner kid.**

In fall 2008, 51 dodgeball teams and around 90 kickball teams competed for bragging rights and the prestigious Kennedy Cup (named for the original dodgeball venue at McMenamins Kennedy School). **Game on!**

By Kevin Perlas, Director of User Experience, Pinpoint Logic

Photo courtesy of Ryan Fleming | Design - Rosy Harris

LADD HOUSE

    I did a double-take, one warm fall morning, while walking in the Park Blocks to the PSU Farmers' Market. A house was moving down the street. And not just any house. The historic 1883 Ladd Carriage House was making its way back to the corner of SW Broadway and Columbia. Today it was being restored to its former location by an architectural firm with a plan for restoring and recycling the building for future owners. I thought the house had been demolished and replaced with a parking garage and a modern building.

    As I walked to the market, with tears in my eyes and a lump in my throat, I turned to my friend and said, "Only in Portland." Inspired by Jerry Bosco and Ben Milligan, founders of the Architectural Heritage Center, Portlanders seem to have a great passion for historic preservation. Appreciation for craftsmanship and the importance of recycling abounds. Where else can you find places like Rejuvenation, The Rebuilding Center, and Hippo Hardware?

    Only in Portland.

Written, photographed and designed by Julie Almquist
www.AlmquistProductions.com

"When you strip away the rhetoric, preservation is simply having the good sense to hold on to things that are well designed, that link us with our past in a meaningful way, and that have plenty of good use left in them."

- Richard Moe, President
National Trust for Historic Preservation

On a brisk morning walk, several months ago on Forest Park's wide Holman Lane, a friend and I disturbed a napping coyote in grassy Holman Meadow. Kate and I were engrossed in conversation while walking up the gentle grade when a lone coyote sauntered out of the high grass onto the trail. She stretched with a yawn, looked over her shoulder beyond her tail, then turned around, seeming to have acknowledged us, and nonchalantly strolled up the trail. She was not more than twenty-five feet ahead of us. Surprised, Kate and I stopped and looked at each other. Then simultaneously we wondered aloud if either could remember reports of coyotes sleeping in the meadow. After a few more steps, our bold coyote stepped a bit more quickly and disappeared around a bend in the trail.

Wild Creatures
COME TO THE CITY

By Francie Royce, Active Volunteer and Freelance Writer

There are numerous stories like this about wild coyotes coming into the city; stories that circulate around our neighborhood, tucked into the edge of Forest Park in Portland's Northwest Hills. And I love it that there are many more. Forest Park, often bragged about by Portlanders as the largest undeveloped park within a city's limits, has miles of trails and no swing sets or playground. To call it a park is confusing to children for whom the word "park" means swings and slides. It's really a forest in the city.

Sometimes the forest releases its wild creatures to the surrounding neighborhoods. Neighbors often hear a concert of yipping and barking at night or see coyotes in the day or night. Several months can go by with no sightings of the wily creatures, then hand-scribbled signs on telephone poles that "Kitty is missing" start appearing and it's obvious that coyotes are back in the area. One neighbor, whose yard backs up to the boundary of the park, gets bushy-tailed visitors sunning themselves like household pet dogs just outside his windows. Another neighbor gets coyotes coming into his yard to sniff around an animal sculpture. One sunny day, I looked out my front door to see a furry animal lounging in a sunny spot on the street pavement at the Aspen trailhead. After a double-take, it wasn't a neighbor's dog after all. Occasional cars would drive slowly past while the coyote would languorously raise his head only to lay it back down, undisturbed, as he continued soaking up the rays. Another time, as I rode my bike down the hill early in the morning, a coyote trotted up the hill, presumably after a night of kitty hunting, back into Forest Park, maybe to nap in the high grasses of Holman Meadow.

Design by Krissy Gilhooly
Coyote photo by Charlie Metcalf

45

OLD PORTLAND

When I walk through the oldest part of town, from Second Avenue down to Front (many Portlanders will call it nothing else), I see old buildings, but what I look for is a lost city; the first Portland. That city, with its riverfront downtown, cast-iron facades, Italianate mansions, Chinatown, and crowded mast-filled harbor has almost entirely vanished.

The first Portland was as unique as it was isolated. The Willamette was its lifeline to the rest of the world. As its 1880s apogee coincided with the height of cast-iron's popularity as a building material, its blocks of ornate facades bespoke ambition, refinement and prosperity when Seattle was a rapidly expanding maze of kindling. On the West Coast, only San Francisco had more cast-iron architecture — that is, until April 18th 1906.

By the 1890s, that riverfront city was already on the wane. Downtown moved inland as streetcars pushed the city outward and architecture changed. A century of demolition, freeway construction, bridge approaches and a seawall along the river erased most of the original downtown.

Old Portland's residents are even more elusive than its remnants. It is easy enough to track down idealized biographies of founders and notables, but what of the thousands of others who shared its streets and dreams? There is little left to tell us about who they were.

Or is there? Their city, with a streetcar line on First, with its breweries and no less than three beer gardens; a city that fostered the activism of proto-suffragette Abigail Scott Duniway and a strong do-it-yourself ethic (even most of the cast-iron was manufactured locally); a city with bookstores, coffee and, at one point, a mania for bike riding, might seem familiar.

When I walk through what little remains of the first Portland, I try to reconstruct it in my mind. It is not easy. The past is an alien place. Then it strikes me, maybe there is more to old Portland than cast-iron buildings that survives.

For an instant I can almost see a lost city.

This small building, at 233 SW Front Street, is one of the remaining 20 or so examples of Portland's iron-cast architecture that originally dominated its riverfront downtown. Depending on the source, it was built in 1870 or 1885. Next to it is Portland's oldest commercial building, albeit heavily modernized, the Hallock & McMillan building, built prior to the Civil War in 1857.

BY DAN HANECKOW

DESIGN BY STUART HAURY

Springtime

and then, dying, a deep purple. It's time of the rain and gloom of winter, I begin to dream of spring, to crave of coming. Generally, all the trillium have disappeared by May 1st. Occasionally, I see someone picking a trillium on daily walks in Forest Park. This lily and cannot help but blurt of the Forest is a wildflower out "Don't you know that if that thrives in soil enriched by you pick a trillium, it won't the decaying trees and the grow again for seven years?" luxuriant mat of our temperate. I am not actually sure this is rain forest, bringing joy to all botanically true, but the scold those open to receiving renewal in we can't let from nature the trillium's three this insult to nature petals, the trilogy of many pass unchallenged. religions, symbolizes rebirth.

Its wanton picking reflects the I have seen the first bud selfishness in all of us that pushing through the earth wants to expropriate beauty, to unveil its white to own it for ourselves. flower against an The natural world is understory of three green, full of splendor, heart-shaped leaves as early as free and bountiful, but we can February 25, and almost never neither possess nor recklessly later than March 10th. harvest such magnificence Neighbors in Willamette Heights, without destroying our a community abutting Forest environment and a sustainable Park, raise their Trillium Flag in future for proud defiance of the still soggy our children. spring immediately on report of the first trillium sighting. The season of the trillium lasts two weeks, with late arrivals thrusting upwards as the first bloom travel mature.

words by Michael Royce
Energy Consultant and Founder, Green Empowerment
www.greenempowerment.org

Design by Kathleen Grebe

47

BILL

by Steve Gronert Ellerhoff

designed by gabrielle drinard

BILL comes to visit me nearly every day at the wind-ups counter.

"where's the peewee," he'll ask my coworkers on his way into the store. while i organize and restock the finest in chinese plastic and gearation, he appears, shuffling in my direction without aid from the two canes he carries in one hand.

he shares tales of the horses he had down in klamath falls, his favorite an appaloosa, and shows up the next day wearing his old gear: a knee-length sheepskin coat, a dusty and crooked black felt hat with a wide brim, and his spurs jangling in a grocery sack.

"what's new?" i always ask, and he always says, "oh, an african critter with horns 'n' a beard."

some days we go through the cards in his wallet: lifetime memberships to the Association of US Model Railroad Enthusiasts, the NRA, the American Handball Association. some days he has a handball with him and challenges me to a game at the court, threatening a trouncing, bouncing the ball and catching it with his spry old hand. there are stories of his children and their children, especially his granddaughter who stands six foot eight and his son who's a psychiatrist in switzerland. sometimes he needs to sit and, on occasion, his leg slightly out of joint, he asks me to yank on his foot to set it back—which i do, knelt before him like a shoe salesman-cum-physical therapist.

he speaks of the seen and unseen, of his out-of-body service in the navy during wwII, of his being chairman of jesus christ's spiritual mafia. and sometimes he brings me artwork.

"here ya go," he says, laying it down like a bartender sets a napkin. "you can keep it if ya want. keep it."

The Portland I Love

by Steve Potestio I was born here. I've left twice to live in other cities. Always came back. The Portland I love is based in roots. The Chinese grocery that sold you beer when you were 16. The stairs going up sides of hills you had to trek up and down to smoke pot and see a matinee. The smell of brewing beer from Blitz Weinhard. The drug dealers at the archery range in Washington Park. The weather ball you watched to see if it was flashing white meaning snow. Sledding down streets. What happens to a basketball when dribbled into a puddle. The difference between rain and showers. The peanut bowl. Gritty Portland. Dirty Portland. The roots of Portland.

DESIGN+PHOTOS: JAMES WIGGER
STAIRS PHOTO: STEVE POTESTIO

ADVENTURES ON THE COW TRAIN

HOLD ON TO YOUR BUTTERS.

Twelve miles downstream from town lies Sauvie Island, a local getaway for all types: beach-going nudists, wannabe Tour de France racers, wildlife voyeurs, and carloads of agro-tourists.

Last October, I landed a sweet part-time gig at the Pumpkin Patch, pretending to be a farmer. I drove a little diesel John Deere tractor, towing around the "cow train." The infamous cow train is actually twenty Holstein-pattern-painted, 55-gallon drums, each welded to a two-wheeled axle, and all hitched together, filled with really giddy children, driving "safely" through hordes of pumpkin-hauling tourists.

All went well the first two days.

The last day, after eating lunch with my boss while he explained that the cow train is his biggest liability in the entire operation, all hell broke loose. This particular ride started out the same as always with me hollering "Y'all heifer a good time?" "Hold on to your butters," and "Let's moove out." After the tractor lurched forward under the strain of a full train, we zigzagged through crowds with me yelling "Cow Train, mooooove over." The kids laughed and asked to go faster. Of course I obliged, and we hit the bumps extra fast, clipping the edge of the haunted corn maze. Then I spotted some unsuspecting folks in the crowd and cut the wheel sharp to get the cow train cars to follow the tractor in a loop. This maneuver was usually pretty simple: the cows would follow one another and the riders would get a kick out of me and the tractor approaching the caboose. Only, that particular time, one of the tourists that we rounded up within the circling cow train cars must have been daydreaming.

Long story short, in front of hundreds of onlookers, the last two cows trampled the poor fellow. He was unhurt but udderly embarrassed.

By Scott Latham, Organic Farmer

TWI5T & PLAY

WHERE I LIVE.

TWIST & PLAY SCOOTER CLUB OF PORTLAND, OREGON, IS THE OLDEST ACTIVE SCOOTER CLUB IN THE AREA. THE CLUB IS TWENTY MEMBERS STRONG, ALL FROM VARIOUS BACKGROUNDS AND CAREERS, BUT WITH ONE THING IN COMMON: BIKES. THE SCOOTERS VARY IN PEDIGREE, BUT MOST IN THE CLUB RIDE VINTAGE ITALIAN SCOOTERS. MEMBERS HAVE BEEN RIDING DAILY, RAIN OR SHINE, LONG BEFORE HIGH GAS PRICES CONTRIBUTED TO THEIR BOOM IN POPULARITY. TO THEM IT'S MORE ABOUT A LIFESTYLE, LESS ABOUT A CHEAP WAY TO SAVE GAS. THEY FIX THEIR OWN BIKES, SURF AROUND THE INTERNET FOR PARTS, AND GET TOGETHER ON TUESDAY NIGHTS TO HANG OUT. IT'S A CULTURE THAT PORTLAND EMBRACES AND IT GIVES ME ONE MORE REASON TO LOVE THIS PLACE.

BY BRYAN HOYBOOK-BRYANHOYBOOK.COM
DESIGN BY TROY STANGE

51

PORTLAND SAVED MY LIFE!

I drove to Portland from Des Moines, Iowa, with a car full of possessions and knowing no one.

Moving to Portland was the hardest thing I've ever done. It's a culture shock from the cookie cutter Midwestern life. I've never been so damp. I've also never seen so many shades of green nor smelled air so clean. Portland shook me to my core. I realized quickly that the people who reside here are full of fire and passion. And everyone wants you to share theirs. It forced me to search my own soul to its depths. Early into my time here someone said, "You've got to know who you are and what you stand for or else you'll blow like a reed in the wind." It's true.

There's an independent spirit here and a diversity that is so beautiful. At first it scared and intimidated me. Now it strengthens me. Stereotypically, in living here I have grown a snooty opinion of coffee, of microbrews, of the underdog, a disdain for umbrella use and an even bigger appetite for books. But I've also found me. And as silly as it may sound, I attribute that to Portland. Learning to live, learn and love here completed and awakened me.

There's a song called "Objects of My Affection," by Peter, Bjorn and John, that has become my Portland song.

The chorus goes:
"And the question is, was I more alive then than I am now?
I happily have to disagree;
I laugh more often now, I cry more often now,
I am more me."

by April Hauck

design and painting by elizabeth avakian

Portland Streets by C.J. White

I'm writing in regards to what I now consider my unconditional love for Portland. Since my arrival here in the summer of 2006, my life has changed on an epic level. Within a year of arriving here, I became a volunteer and employee for the Julia West House (a day center for homeless and low income people). I've received the Humanity in Perspective scholarship granted through the Oregon Council for the Humanities and Reed College; have been both a columnist and contributor to Street Roots; have been published in two Write About Portland anthologies; have had a showing featuring my poetry and mixed media at Warner Pacific College; and performed a lead role at the haunted attraction Fright Town. My work with the Julia West House continues, and I have been hosting a monster movie club called "The Monster Piece Theatre" there weekly.

So here is the twist....

Since I have arrived, I have lived outdoors in downtown Portland, sleeping under an overpass between a stone pillar and a cobweb-embellished wrought iron fence. With the exception of one self-published zine, and my humble job, I never have money because Portland provides what little needs I have, thus far. She also has been my muse with my shared words and provided me a vast canvas illustrated through a montage of serendipitous acts, experiencing up close and personal the river rats, laughing beavers, dragon boats, zoo bombers with beer-scented sleeping bags, drug addicts, perverts, gratuitous goose poop, angry raccoons, folk singers, fire dancers, cross dressers, spongy narcolepsy, cranky security guards, mean drunks, despondent body odors, aggressive panhandlers, petitioners, bongo-wielding hippies, street poets, tweakers, secondhand smoke, food poisoning, Bigfoot, rain & roses, and the small commas of thoughtlessness that follow my dreams each morning I wake up in her embrace. The white noise of the 405 reminding me of an early tide and a late kiss blown from a ghost in a tranquility I call Portland.

Page design and illustration: Rochelle Koivunen

THE CHILDREN'S GARDEN MURAL IS 16'X4' AND ITS VIBRANT COLORS DEPICT CHILDREN PLANTING SEEDS AND NURTURING THE GARDEN.

The City of Lake Oswego believes that investing in spaces for our youth is important for the community. This is apparent in the City's foresight when it purchased a former dairy farm and created a park with a Children's Garden. The eight 20'x20' plots that make up the Children's Garden at Luscher Farm create an outdoor classroom for children of all ages to explore and learn. Classes, camps, clubs, and youth programs share the space year 'round. Kids plant seeds, tend the strawberry patch, harvest beans from inside a teepee, and have pizza parties with veggies from the pizza plot.

Art created by the children is an important aspect in the garden because it maintains the space as theirs. They tend the space just as they tend the seedlings and they grow together.

The Children's Garden Mural was painted by a volunteer muralist and youth garden volunteers.

LAKE OSWEGO

GROW

Words: Hilary Lowenberg, Former Children's Garden Coordinator

Design: Yvonne Perez Emerson, Cre8tivegirl

Cut, fold and glue to create your own seed packet!

I love the lettuce that grows in my backyard.

Portland has the best growing climate—even if you don't think you can grow food, the soil tells a different story.

I live near Mount Tabor; ancient volcanic ash is embedded in my backyard. I run my fingers through it, listening.

I hear the whisper of a universe conspiring in my favor.

I hear myself, believing.

By Janet Freeman

Design: Gail Weiss

55

I SAID MY GOODBYES to my fellow writers at the Write Around Portland group and headed down Burnside toward Powell's bookstore to catch the streetcar home. As I approached the corner of 10th and Burnside, I heard music and singing wafting through the air. I turned the corner and was bombarded by the song, "You Ain't Nothin' but a Hound Dog." And there in front of me was Elvis, albeit an impersonator. Even though he wasn't the real King, he did bring back fond memories of that era long ago: cruising, drive-ins, chicks and — ah! — rock and roll, the 50s, a time to be alive.

Despite this unexpected invitation to trip down memory lane, my first inclination was to continue walking down 10th Avenue, to avoid eye contact with this impersonator of my idol. It was late, I was tired, and I guess too cheap to give the obligatory monetary tip. Besides, I had a streetcar to catch. But suddenly I stopped, an undeniable warmth washing over me. I know I smiled. Even though my pulsating friend on the corner was not the real King, I thought he should be rewarded for making this old man happy for a short time. I reached in my wallet and pulled out a dollar and retraced my steps to where "Elvis" was still singing. I tossed the dollar into his hat on the ground and got a "high five" from "my man," and then I headed for the streetcar.

One thing I love about Portland is, you never know who might be right around the corner. Maybe Marilyn Monroe, Frankenstein or Count Dracula.

I CAN'T WAIT TO SEE WHAT HAPPENS TOMORROW.

Words by **Dan Peski**; Design by **Alicia Nagel**; Elvis photo © Ben Garland, bengarland.com

" SHAKE, RATTLE & ROLL "

BREAKFAST JOINTS

If you've spent more than a month in Portland and you haven't been to at least three breakfast joints, then you really need to reevaluate what you're doing with your life.

While living off NW 23rd, I found myself regularly ending up at the Stepping Stone Cafe, simply because it was two blocks closer than Besaws.

Their ever-changing ceiling decor consists of action figures on strings that shake, rattle and roll in lockstep with the door and random pullings from the staff.

These dangling figures keep me entertained and kick more ass than your favorite summer action flick.

'Breakfast Joints' *was written by Chris Alan. Photography and design by Simon Black, except bottom left, by the author.*

Stepping Stone Cafe poached eggs and bacon will set you back $7.75.

57

CATTITUDE

The Clackamas Community Cat Club (CCCC) strives to create Cat-Based Art in a supportive, loving environment. Through interactive workshops, community building and outreach, we hope to create a cozy catmosphere for all feline friends.

The Cattitude Dance Ensemble is the performance arm of the Clackamas Community Cat Club. The troupe was established in the winter of 2006 as representative of our love of felines and as a response to cat injustices that we have seen in our community. We, as Cattitude, feel that we can make an impact on cat owners, cat allies, and even cat skeptics, with our dance performances.

DANCIN' CATS

As a dance troupe, we attempt to work with as many dance styles as possible. In the past, we have performed jazz dance, ballet, modern, and even studied a little fire dance.

Cattitude has now performed in Portland, Seattle, and across the Midwest, bringing our form of cuddly cat art to the masses. In the works for the future is the CBA, or Cat-Based Art Festival, slated to occur in the fall of '09.

Check us out online at www.myspace.com/cattitudedanceensemble

by Jodi Kansagor

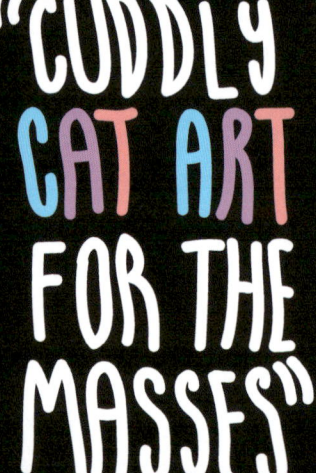

> "CUDDLY CAT ART FOR THE MASSES"

SKINNY WHITE MAN

By Lisa Parsons: Writer, Visual Artist

Portland's Time-Based Art Festival, run by PICA, is one thing that makes Portland bold and on the edge. This ten-day festival is a convergence of contemporary performance, dance, theater, visual art, film, and music that isn't afraid to go beyond the boundary of the absurd. The late night club, THE WORKS, brings out bawdy, nasty events like The Neal Medlyn Experience Live!, a faithful re-creation of Beyonce's 2007 hit concert DVD, The Beyonce Experience Live! Such intensity and fluff at the same time. This skinny, white man from Texas strutted and moaned and brought me to the verge of virtual insanity. Delicious and amorphous – costumes coming and going all the time.

Designer: Drew Cone

PORTLAND PERFECTION

Strange as it may seem, I love the weather in Portland. Fall, with its soft languorous sunny days, gradually paints the trees crimson and yellow, colors that linger into December. Yellow leaves slowly drift from the elms onto the piles of pumpkins and pears in the farmer's market where the earthy scent of roasting peppers floats through the warm yet cool air.

Sure it's dark, cold and wet in winter, but the grass stays green and bulbs coming up are our New Year's gifts. Once in a while we have a beautiful big snow, which the young daffodils don't mind as much as drivers. Shorts show up during the February thaw and then we dash among "sunbreaks," coax gardens, walk dogs, run, and ride bikes through the dazzling green canvas splashed with evermore colors of spring. In February, crocuses and daffodils reward us for our patience, followed shortly by tulips and azaleas, and it isn't even April yet.

They say it always rains at Rose Festival in early June, and mostly they are right...except when the sun shines all month long and we wonder why that myth lives on. July, August, September, we call "Portland Perfection." Bluest sky, sun and breezes every day, no humidity, no rain and next to no bugs. And then it starts again.

Eloise Damrosch

june o underwood
www.juneunderwood.com

I'm an oil painter, plein air, who likes to set up in my Buckman neighborhood, in southeast Portland. Southeast has a lot of characters, in the best sense of the word. **I was painting at the intersection of SE Alder & 6th Avenue one day.** That corner has good history– the Eastside Funeral Directors headquarters & mortuary is now the Volunteers of America building; the Odd Fellows IOOF Orient Lodge No. 17 is occupied by a going-out-of-business-but-legendary The Office Supply Co.; the Melody Ballroom & Rivers of Life Church, on the northeast corner, was a Woodsmen of America structure. Only the US Bank parking lot lacks interest, although the backsides of the buildings behind it are interestingly wonky. As I painted on that corner, a Hispanic man, about my height, approached me, smiling broadly.

"Do you speak English?" he asked. "Yes," I said, slightly puzzled.

"Is this the U. S. of A.? I ask you, are we in the U. S. of A.?" He was a bit insistent & also a bit flirtatious. I was a bit wary.

"Last time I looked, it was Portland, Oregon, which is indeed in the U. S. of A."

"Never, never, never," he said, pulling himself up to his full height, "have I seen a painter on a corner in the U. S. of A." & he beamed at me. I couldn't help but beam back. Then he hit me up for a buck for a bus ticket.

When I said I had no money with me, he wasn't at all upset. We chatted about the weather & painting outside & that particular street corner & its buildings. As he walked away, he turned & said something in a language I don't speak. I suddenly felt uneducated. But in the middle of his fluency of words, I recognized "Picasso" and knew he was doing some kind of artistic comparison, probably in a complimentary way. I raised my hands helplessly and said, "I speak only English."

He laughed & said, "Have a beautiful day, profesora," and went on his way down the street, toward SE Morrison, where I hope he got his buck for the bus. That's the kind of encounter that makes me love painting on the streets of Portland, Oregon, in the U. S. of A.

design by gerry blakney

61

IN THE SEWING UNIVERSE,

50¢ **9785**
PRINTED PATTERN

BUST **34** SIZE **7**

PORTLAND, OREGON,
is affectionately known as the fabric store capital of the world.

PATTERN C

I can attest to this fact, having spent countless happy hours perusing the vast offerings of the local fabric market. The quality and quantity of our textile and notions resources are what make Portland a destination city for fabric store shopping tours and sewing vacation workshops.

As a native Oregonian steeped in the individualism, self-reliance and thrift of the earliest settlers, I have inherited the independent ethos representative of our regional character. Portland's early development of textile and apparel industries was initiated through the pioneering spirit of innovation and the responsible use of natural resources. These fundamental values remain a profound influence in our city's vibrant and diverse creative culture, extending into the sustainability movement, which promotes locally produced products and supports the uniqueness inherent to the natural capital of handcrafted industries.

My relationship with fibers and fabrics reaches back into my earliest childhood memories. It began with finger knitting and hand-stitchery. I was surrounded by women well-versed in the arts of knitting, crocheting, tatting, embroidery and sewing; it was a taken-for-granted feature of my formative years and I absorbed much at my grandmother's knee. It was she who taught me to sew and instilled in me the importance of being precise. She had an eye for detail and a love of excellence. Her words, **"TAKE THE TIME TO DO YOUR BEST WORK—IF IT'S WORTH DOING, IT'S WORTH DOING WELL,"** live in me and have influenced my creative life in innumerable ways.

The nearly inexhaustible supply of fabric resources available in Portland has sustained my life-long interest in apparel design and construction. This extensive experience, coupled with the do-your-own-thing spirit of Portland, led to my work in a new art medium of fabric mosaics. My intuitive understanding of the relationships among color, texture and design, combined with my passion for detail and devotion to technical mastery, makes fabric mosaic the natural medium for my artistic expressions. Living in the fabric store capital of the world has been good for me; it is both source and supplier of my inspiration.

C

A   B   C

author | kerri jones, remnantWorks
designer | marisa d. green, studio danae

p:ear
creatively mentoring homeless youth

I love Portland because of its openness to change, because of its passion and commitment.

It was in the financial slump of 2001 and we were sitting outside at the Brasserie Montmartre (now defunct or in perpetual renewal depending on who you talk to), three unemployed women, three glasses of wine and one big plan.

We had just lost our jobs along with thousands of other Oregonians. The Salvation Army Greenhouse, an agency providing services for homeless kids, was dying off in pieces and one of the first to go was the school where the three of us taught the G.E.D. Now Greenhouse School was closed and it was a palpable loss, both for our students and us. Could we mold what we were grieving and what we had learned into a new form? Could we raise a phoenix from those ashes? And just how many glasses of wine would that take?

Turns out it took a lot. Beth Burns, Pippa Arend and I spent that summer trying to understand what had taken place for us on the corner of 8th and Oak, over a combined 12 years of working with homeless youth. We were trying to figure out what could and should go forward into a new program and what needed to be left in the past. We came up with a few things:

* Everyone deserves dignity and respect
* Relationships--not programs--foster change
* We all have intellectual, emotional and physical needs. We want to meet those daily needs
* No one should go hungry
* Everyone has the right to a toothbrush
* Events don't define people, attitudes do. Attitudes can change

Back to the table in front of the Brasserie Montmartre. The conversation may have gone something like this:

Beth: Ok, we can run a kick-ass day program, but we need somewhere to do it.

Joy: Where would we be if we could be anywhere we wanted?

Practically in one voice: There! (Pointing katty-corner to the long abandoned Cornelius Hotel, AKA Johnny Sole, AKA Rich's Cigar Shop in previous incarnations.)

Beth: But the building's for sale, we only want one floor, need to rent, and no one has been in it since it flooded two years ago.

Pippa: I'll call. Maybe they'll be willing to rent.

They were.

Did we have a business plan? Did we know the statistics connected with new ventures? Did we have financial partners? Were we even aware of the financial climate of the times? Well, sure, on the last one; we'd just been laid off, remember? What we did have was a vision, heart, and each other. And we were in Portland. Apparently it was enough.

Portland has been gracious to p:ear, which has now been in existence for seven years meeting the intellectual, emotional and physical needs of Portland's homeless and transitional kids. I believe p:ear couldn't have come into existence in any other city. p:ear has recently moved from its original location at 801 SW Alder to 338 NW 6th. To meet the need.

By Joy Cartier, Assistant Director p:ear
www.pearmentor.org

> What we did have was a vision, heart, and each other. And we were in Portland. Apparently it was enough.

design by Angela Reat, artwork by p:ear youth

PORTLAND IS A RESTLESS, CREATIVE CITY THAT DOES THINGS LIKE PUT RESTAURANTS IN PINK HOUSES AND MUSIC STUDIOS AND BARS IN OLD REVIVAL CHURCHES; WHERE WE PURSUE THE RELIGION OF WARM PEOPLE, FOOD, AND DRINK, AS WELL AS REFUGE FROM RAINY DAYS, LEST THE WATER CLEANSE OUR IMAGINATIONS TOO THOROUGHLY.

WORDS AND PHOTO BY CHRIS KRUELL | DESIGN BY BRIAR LEVIT

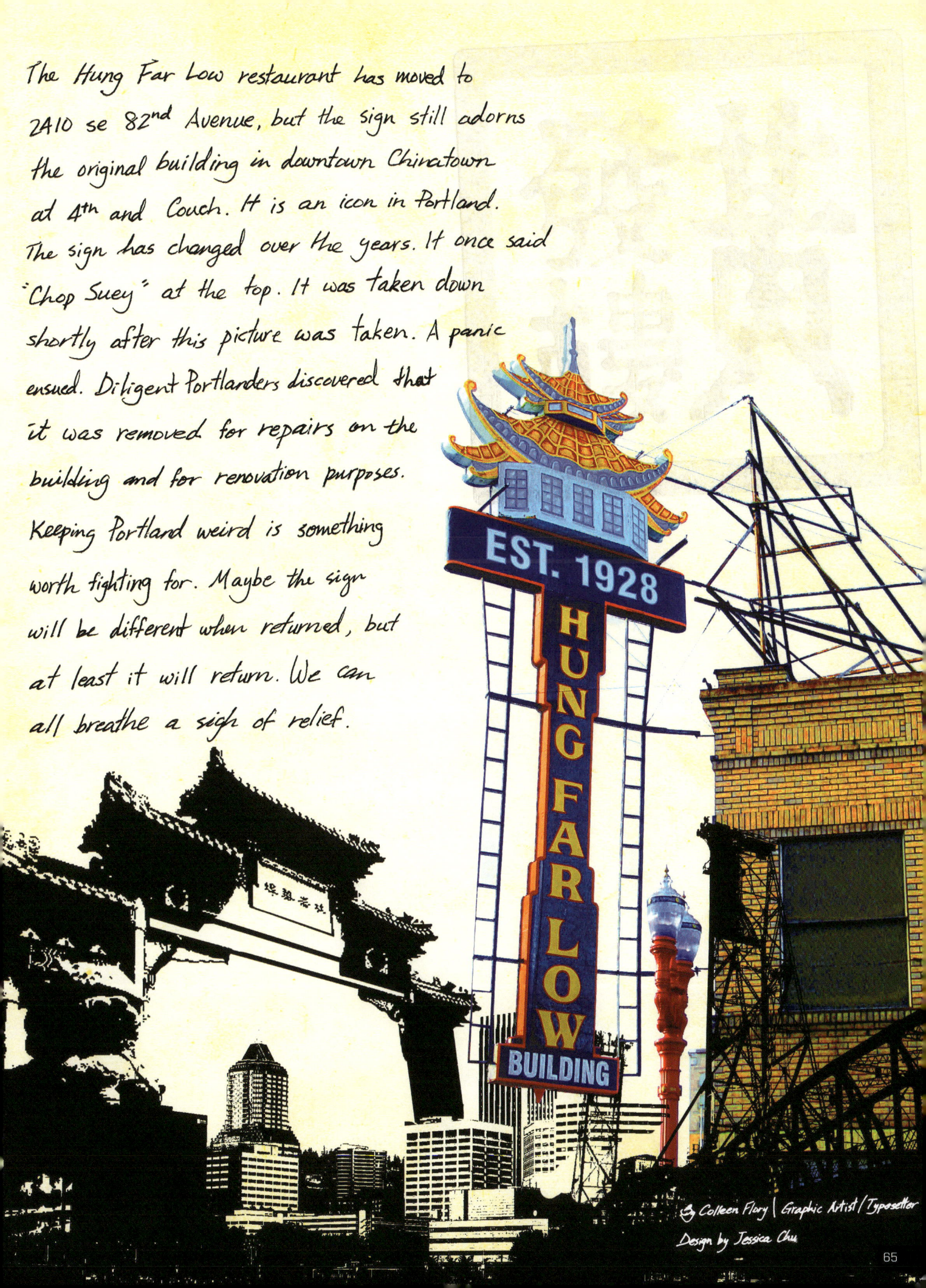

The Hung Far Low restaurant has moved to 2410 SE 82nd Avenue, but the sign still adorns the original building in downtown Chinatown at 4th and Couch. It is an icon in Portland. The sign has changed over the years. It once said "Chop Suey" at the top. It was taken down shortly after this picture was taken. A panic ensued. Diligent Portlanders discovered that it was removed for repairs on the building and for renovation purposes. Keeping Portland weird is something worth fighting for. Maybe the sign will be different when returned, but at least it will return. We can all breathe a sigh of relief.

By Colleen Flory | Graphic Artist / Typesetter
Design by Jessica Chu

PORTLAND SKATEBOARDING

Californians--they're always saying,
"HOW CAN YOU LIVE THERE? IT RAINS ALL THE TIME."
This is good, because it means the secret's kept.

Portland cultivates one of the most electric skateboarding scenes on the West Coast. Sure, water pours down from the sky for months straight--but the winter is, perhaps, when Portland's at its realest. All those out-of-town couch crashers go home to their sunny cities and we have the place to ourselves for cloudy-day sessions and big ramp jams in sweaty, dusty garages. These indoor constructions are scattered like secret jewels across the east side. If you know someone who knows someone, you're in.

Then the spring shines down on us in the form of bright March days, when the dogwoods push out their flowered canopy and we jump in our cars to go find the parks. Beaverton, Tigard, Gabriel, Pier, Glen Haven--massive concrete masterpieces built by real northwest skateboarders.

Eventually, summer's in full swing, and the days are long and hot--and so much to do. Downtown ledges, gaps, and wallride spots in the shadow of skyscrapers. Abandoned warehouses sheltering DIY concrete transition. Weird, skateable industrial stuff like fullpipes and funnels. Secret pools. And of course, Burnside--where there's always something doing. Someone ripping, and someone drunkenly yelling in the background. A dog barking. A group of sweat-drenched dudes headed off to dunk in the river.

Finally, autumn hits--brilliant, coolish days when the kids go back to school and leave the parks empty. Yeah, some of the best shredding of the year happens in the fall. Ah, Portland. If you're a skateboarder, this is the place.

BY JENNIFER SHERROWSKI
WRITER,
SKATEBOARDER,
ET CETERA

page designed by Wendell Walker

Partly Cloudy With A Chance Of Rain 2

I am in my 35th NW winter in Portland. Some years I complain: "Matt Zaffino, I curse you and your 'Light showers' or 'Partly cloudy with a slight chance of rain'!" Or denial strikes: "True Oregonians don't need an umbrella. Rain is a lifestyle like coffee and laundry." This year I appreciate the rain. It means a chance to hike Miss K in Tryon Creek and breathe in the rich earthy scent of the forest floor. Rain is what feeds this place. Portland is the space I call home.

Elizabeth Perlas
Artist, Mom, and dog owner
sugapress.etsy.com • Portland, OR

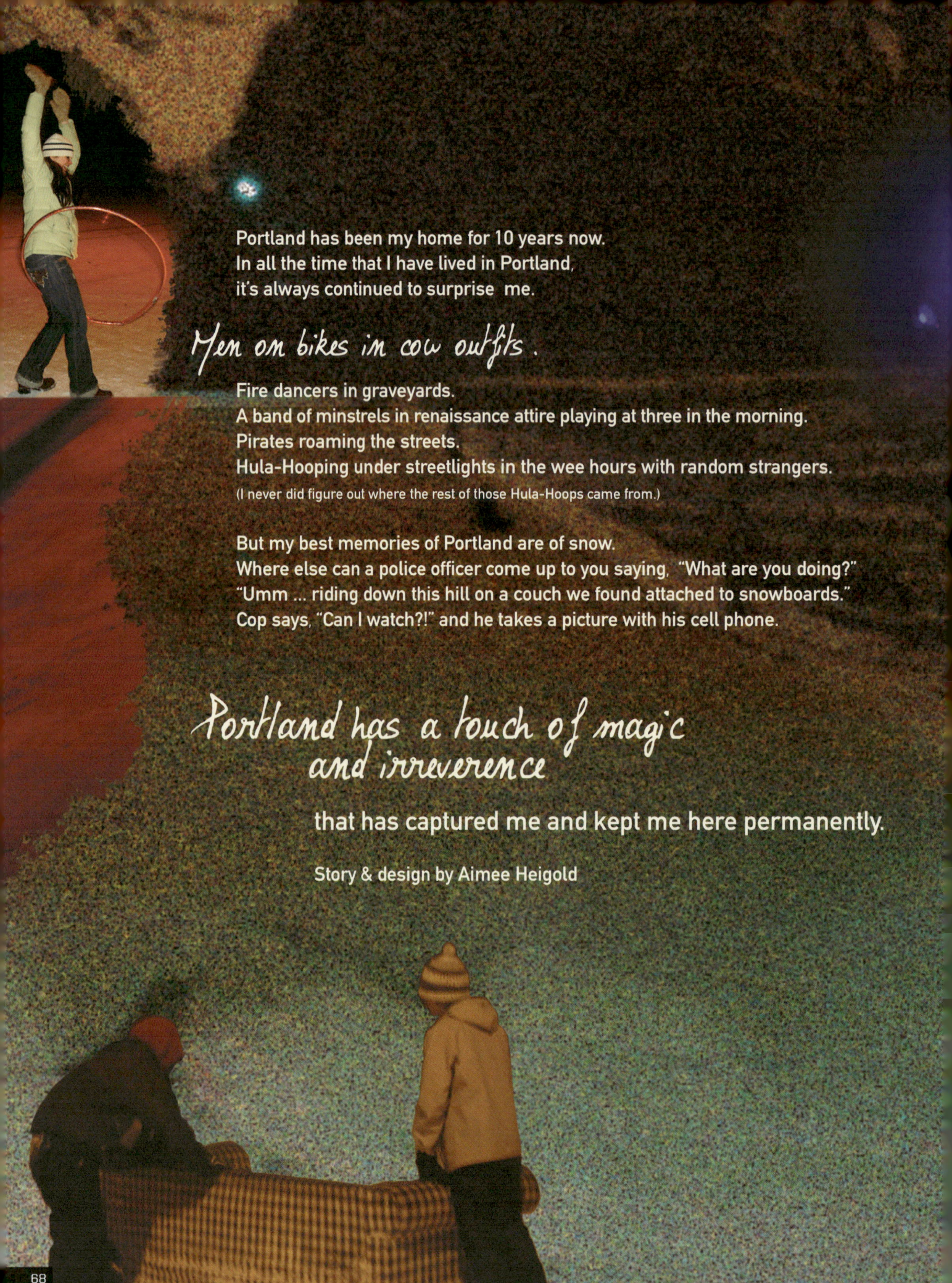

Portland has been my home for 10 years now.
In all the time that I have lived in Portland,
it's always continued to surprise me.

Men on bikes in cow outfits.

Fire dancers in graveyards.
A band of minstrels in renaissance attire playing at three in the morning.
Pirates roaming the streets.
Hula-Hooping under streetlights in the wee hours with random strangers.
(I never did figure out where the rest of those Hula-Hoops came from.)

But my best memories of Portland are of snow.
Where else can a police officer come up to you saying, "What are you doing?"
"Umm ... riding down this hill on a couch we found attached to snowboards."
Cop says, "Can I watch?!" and he takes a picture with his cell phone.

Portland has a touch of magic and irreverence

that has captured me and kept me here permanently.

Story & design by Aimee Heigold

"YOU INSPIRED ME TO RIDE SAFE ON GRAND," she says. I HAD BOUGHT A **BICYCLES ALLOWED FULL LANE STICKER** at CITYBIKES, SO I WAS RIDING AROUND ASSERTING MY RIGHTS + FEELING PROUD. but I had a few drinks while watching the Obama-McCain debate at ROOTS, so what she said didn't quite catch.

"WHAT DOES THAT MEAN?"

"Riding on the street," she says. AT THE INTERSECTION ON STARK, SHE CAME OFF THE SIDEWALK AND PULLED UP NEXT TO ME.

"It's much better. We're allowed the lane, after all."

YOU INSPIRED ME to RIDE SAFE ON GRAND

I DECIDE NOT TO TELL HER ABOUT ALL THE GOOD TIMES I'VE HAD ON GRAND. ABOUT THE CAR OF BLONDES THAT YELLED AT ME TO "USE THE BIKE LANE!" (THERE IS NO BIKE LANE) OR ABOUT THE FATHER IN THE FAMILY VAN THAT TAILED ME FOR BLOCKS UNTIL THE 84 ON RAMP, WHERE HE FELT IT APPROPRIATE TO HONK + FLIP ME OFF. OR ABOUT THE MAN WITH OKLAHOMA PLATES ON HIS FORD CLUB WAGON THAT, LATE ONE FRIDAY NIGHT, NEARLY SIDESWIPED ME. WE WERE THE ONLY TWO PEOPLE ON THE ROAD FOR BLOCKS. I WAS PREPARED TO BASH HIS WINDOWS IN WITH MY U-LOCK, BUT HE SPED AWAY. INSTEAD, I JUST GIVE HER THE THUMBS-UP. BE THE CHANGE, RIGHT?

by: Richard Mavis
photo + illustration by Jacqueline Bos

PORTLAND is **WORLD-RENOWNED** for its **BEER**. The beer is covered in countless blogs, newspapers, and on television. We have **FESTIVALS, TASTINGS**, and we even **DEVOTE** the entire month of July to craft beer. **BREWERS ARE TREATED LIKE CELEBRITIES AND THEY'VE EARNED IT.**

Strip away the glamour, though, and you're left with **HARD WORK** and long hours. Everyone I meet in my journeys thru the **PORTLAND BEER SCENE** wants to be a brewer — until they see what it's actually like for a day in a brewery.

It's HOURS OF CLEANING, LIFTING, MORE CLEANING, MORE LIFTING, and then finishing up with a lot of cleaning. Before the water is even **boiled**, a brewer must decide what's going into their beer. It takes **CREATIVITY** in recipe formulation as well as **KNOWLEDGE** and **EXPERIENCE**, to know what these ingredients will be like in the finished product, usually weeks away.

IT IS THIS MIXTURE OF HARD WORK, CREATIVITY, AND EXPERIENCE that exemplifies this formula for **PORTLAND'S SUCCESSFUL BEER SCENE**.

Written By Matt J. Winter, Editor, www.portlandbeer.org
Design by Stuart Haury

Coffee shops are a haven in Portland for the creative minds with laptops. I especially love the Albina Press on Hawthorne. It is an engaging place to gather, powered by Stumptown Coffee and free Wi-Fi. Looking out the big bright windows, you can catch a glimpse of Mount Tabor.

— LUIS PONCE DE LEON
{DESIGNED BY CARRIE HOOVER}

PIONEER COURTHOUSE ★SQUARE★

overcast and bustling with food carts at lunch hour, or dark and alive with Christmas Lights,

Accuardi's Pizza in Old Town and Sunday Dim Sum in nearby Chinatown,

all-ages shows at matinee the Crystal Ballroom,

RECORD STORES, drugstores, porn stores, art house movie theaters and multiplexes, dirty public bathrooms, opera, ballet and traveling shows at the (then) Civic Auditorium,

a hundred local coffee shops, and the Holy See of our faith, Powell's City of Books.

We were crazy, stupid suburban kids longing for a first taste of something outside our bedrooms and school halls

and the 57 bus from the west-side towns opened up the world to our eager young eyes.

By David Metzger

POWELL'S BOOKS
USED & NEW BOOKS

written by emma burke + designed by stephanie vastakis

One of the many reasons Portland is the best place on Earth

I have lived in Portland my entire life, and even though my favorite places in the city have changed over the course of my thirteen years, there is one location that has a special spot reserved in my heart: Powell's Books. The only place in the city that can keep me captivated for hours, even days, at a time. Walking into Powell's is an adventure fit for any avid reader. You never know what you might find! That limited edition Harry Potter book you couldn't even find on eBay; the next book in a series you have been anticipating for months; a used text book you didn't want to shell out hundreds of dollars for a new copy of; anything in the literary world you can imagine will be waiting for you on the vast plains of Powell's. You just need to look for it. Powell's was the first place I discovered *Maus* by Art Spiegelman, one of the most innovative books I've ever read. Not only that, but Powell's was the very first place I realized I aspired to be a Portland hipster, flaunting my Macbook in local coffee shops while I write my uber creative blog. Powell's Books represents The City of Roses very nicely, old yet hip, calm but often crazy, hilarious and sometimes sad, and most of all, warm and welcoming.

Chinese Garden
by Carole Zoom   carolezoom.com
art . photography . activism

When I moved into a small downtown condo, I left behind an award-winning garden of native plants and unusual perennials that I created from scratch in an unremarkable suburban lot. Gardening had gotten into my blood, and when I arrived in my new home, I adopted the Portland Classical Chinese Garden as my garden.

In lovely summer weather or winter drizzle, I come to the garden twice or three times a week. I sit in the teahouse, sip tea, and watch the garden change. And as their slogan says, it is a different garden every time I visit.

In fall, the Japanese maple near the teahouse turns to a deep carmine; in winter, the persimmons hang tenuously on a bare tree near the water; in summer, a flush of orchids dots the grounds; in spring, the wisteria cascade like tiny grapes over their lovingly manicured vines.

Some days I capture the garden with photos, some days sketches. This woodblock I created to explore my fascination with the plants and architecture of the garden. Though I consider this garden to be mine personally, created for me, y'all are welcome to visit too.

> *"I sit in the teahouse, sip tea, and watch the garden change."*

Designed by Walker Cahall

Portland
holds a very special place in ♥ our hearts ♥

Separately, and from two disparate parts of the country, we each took a risk and moved to Portland in early 2007. Happenstance soon united us; we seized the opportunity and set forth discovering the city -- and ourselves -- together. We went on crazy adventures every weekend, became best friends, and found love.

To us, Portland is not a city. It is our moment in time. A juncture in life where we were able to unravel ourselves, meet lovely people, see beautiful places, and make future plans.

We realized our mutual desire there: To live a more sustainable life, and show others that they can do it, too. In Portland, there are many elements of sustainability already in motion, and tons of people to make it happen.

Although we love the thought of living our lives in the Pacific Northwest, we realize that we can make a bigger difference on the opposite end of the country, in rural north Georgia. We have plans to build an earthen home, live off the grid, and start an organic farm.

Our dream is just beginning. See it all happen at ourfarmadventure.org

BG + LB

-Ben Garland and Laura Bentz

L hugged B right here, seconds after meeting for the first time. :)

Our first ride was around Mount Hood in the freezing cold!

LSB

Dear Laura,
This is my heart → ♡ and I give it to YOU.
ALWAYS ALWAYS ALWAYS
Love → Your Ben

REDWOOD NATIONAL PARK
I love you with all my heart

Blissful relaxation on a bench at Mount Tabor.

Scooter loves you and so do I! I can't wait until we build our own house together. We will sit on the porch and watch the sun go down while a fresh cherry pie bakes in the oven ☺
You are the best!
♡ B

Safety vest B bought L for visibility while motorcycle riding.

Fake roach from "Aunt Mary's" in Lincoln City, OR

<3 I am a bird. Sometimes I am in the tree. Sometimes I am with you.

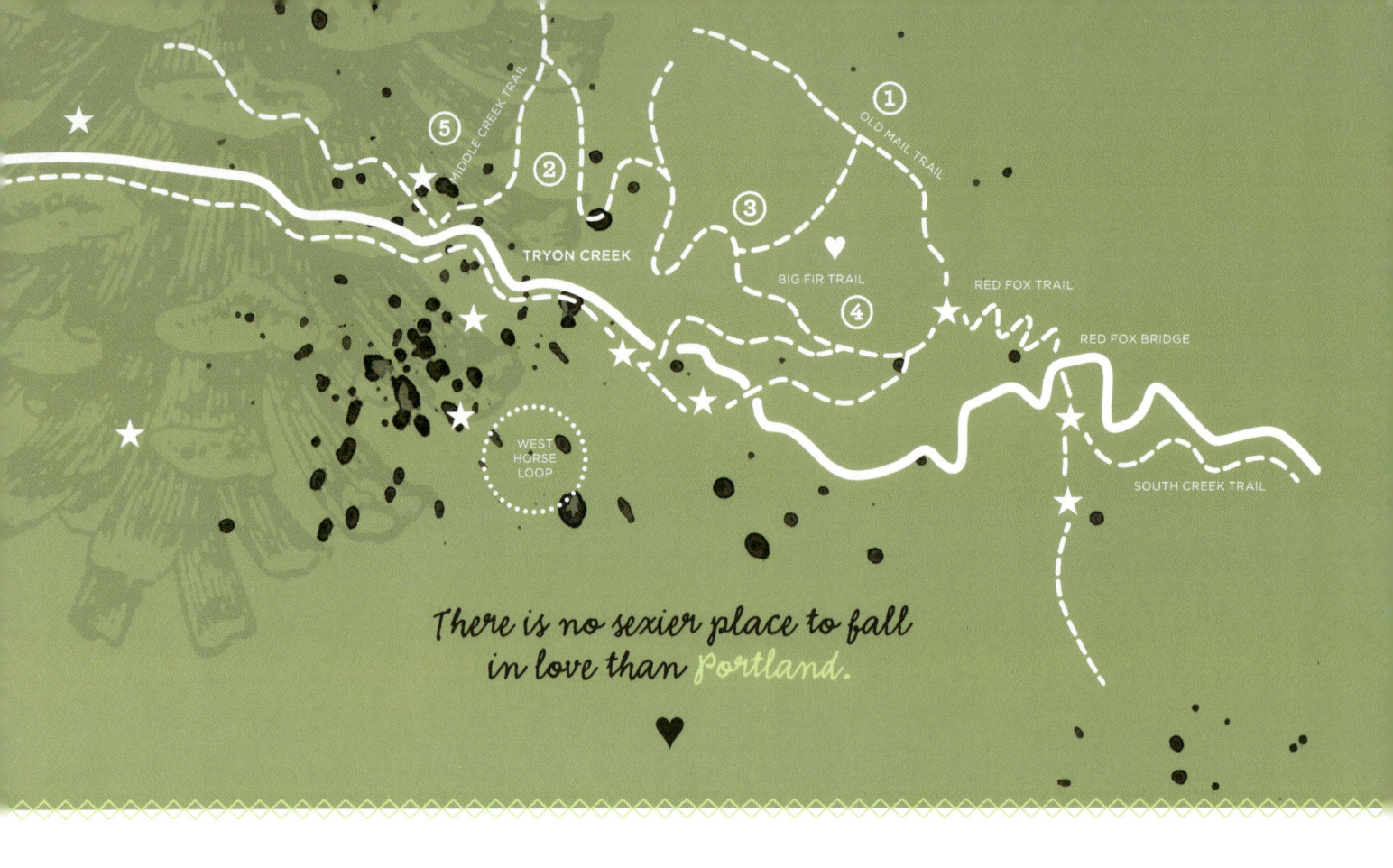

There is no sexier place to fall in love than Portland.

❤

For outdoorsy types, there is no sexier place to fall in love than Portland. My first date with my future husband, we took a walk in Tryon Creek. It was December, and coldish, but comfortable enough to traipse along the Big Fir Trail. My husband is a native Portlander and a science teacher and on that first auspicious date, amid towering conifers, fecund ferns, and slippery moss, he described to me the difference between Douglas firs and Western hemlocks. *Seriously.* He held the needles up to my face and pointed out their myriad characteristics. Despite this, I went out with him again.

As for me, I am not a native Oregonian, and after a couple of years of hiking, climbing and playing in the woods (which culminated in a recent elopement on Mt. Hood), I still cannot remember the distinguishing needle patterns of our various evergreens. But, it doesn't matter, because whenever we're in the forest, I can count on my loving groom to be my ever-present and stalwart guide.

tryon creek
by Suzy Vitello Soulé, *writer*
designed by Megan Clark

lone fir cemetery

by tiffany lee brown

You seek solitude. Your Russian family plants flowers on his grave every week. You have nowhere else to sleep or deal drugs. You want to see the city's pioneers; want to walk where Portlanders unceremoniously erected an administrative building over the remains of local Chinese workers; want to stare at the girl's grave, just twelve years old, 1890s, want to wonder: how did she die?

Maybe you're like me. Maybe you come here for solace, for a silent audience to witness your ephemeral acts of environmental art making. Maybe, like me, you come here for the sounds: chatter of squirrels, traffic on Stark Street, planes overhead, fingers of wind in trees. Maybe you're here because you've never before seen a thousand black crows taking flight at once. Do they collide?

DESIGNED BY KRISTIN CASALETTO

SMELLS

When we were in middle school, my sister and I came up with a proposal for a line of room fragrances that we called "Smells Like Portland." It would be a set of spray bottles that captured the scent of the town for the homesick- or extreme-Portlander, and that consisted of:

- FOREST PARK *after a good rain*
- VOODOO DOUGHNUT
- International Rose Test Garden
- SALMON ST. FOUNTAIN
- MUSIC MILLENNIUM (Jazz, Classical, Rock N' Roll)

While our marketing gold mine never came to be (probably for good reason), these places continue to sit with me well into my young adult years as the most distinctive sensory spots that make Portland feel like home. They're part of the charm of a city that thrives on individuality and creativity, where buildings blend seamlessly into parks and the greater landscape. So I guess I'm OK with the fact that my house will never smell like PDX, because it just means I have to get out and experience the city firsthand instead.

And that's nothing to turn your nose up at.

By Jenny Cestnik / Graduate student of Architecture
Designed by Rachel Beyer

I LOVE PORTLAND

for its green spaces, especially the ones designed by Michael Lawrence Halprin.

The first time I walked east on SW Mill, crossing 4th and heading down the stairs, I had no idea that there was a park tucked behind the tall buildings.

Then the path opened up into a little forest, tall trees rising from green grass-covered mounds that mysteriously made the space seem L*A*R*G*E*R. It was a cool summer morning, and sun slanted through the foliage. On the small terrace at the other end of the park, a woman was doing Tai Chi.

Michael Lawrence Halprin designed that quiet woodland place, Pettygrove Park, as well as Ira's Fountain, and the Lovejoy Fountain.

Ira's Fountain, on the block in front of the Keller Auditorium, is the best known of the three, but they are all beautiful, and they are all designed to be used.

When you visit Ira's Fountain, be sure to walk behind the waterfall, and if you've ever read Tolkien, you'll wonder if Michael Lawrence Halprin read him, too.

By Janet Lunde

design + pdx image: heaum

I WAS VISITING FROM ATLANTA. THIS WAS TEN YEARS AGO. IT WAS SUPPOSED TO BE A TEN-DAY VISIT.

I was visiting from Atlanta. This was ten years ago. It was supposed to be a ten-day visit.

One morning, I found this dumpy diner for breakfast, which was a hobby of mine, to find fabulous dumpy diners. At the time, I was slowly creeping my way through an old copy of **The Brothers Karamazov** that I had found in my father's bookshelf. It was taking me forever to read, but I still remember how much I loved it. After I ordered my food, the pretty waitress at this dumpy diner got a look at the cover of my book. "Dostoevsky," she said. "I just read that book last week." She said it as lightly as you would tell someone that you have the exact same unremarkable backpack. She said this to me and then she went back into the kitchen.

DOSTOEVSKY

I don't remember much else about that breakfast (I don't even remember what the tattoos on her arms were all about), but I remember that — before paying the bill — I had decided I wasn't leaving Portland.

By Yuvi Zalkow

Designed by Lindsey Frei

portland bridges

I love the Portland bridges. The angles and curves of Portland steel and Portland iron, the concrete pillars and pilings, hands that hold them up into the Portland sky. The color of them painted red and black and sea breeze green. Close up color of rust and graffiti and painted over patchwork of muted tones. Peeling tongues of color; rust revealing, and Jackson pigeon Pollock splatter patterned brushwork. Driving over them an East West adventure. Driving over them at night; the Steel Bridge a medieval fortress of black towers. Portland bridges ruminate at night over a river dark and shimmering with city lights.

STORY: STEVE SNELL, MEDICAL INSURANCE BILLER   DESIGN: LISA HOLMES, YULAN STUDIO   PHOTOS: STEVE SNELL AND LISA HOLMES

A Heavenly Paddle... Fall on the Tualatin River

To float on the Tualatin River, slow and meandering, awash in the golden sunlight of a late fall afternoon, is heavenly. Nestled as it is in the suburban neighborhoods of Washington and Clackamas counties, you might hardly know the river is there, so close but feeling so far away. A flicker, a kingfisher, a heron… the splash of a fish or the slap of a beaver, these are wondrous sounds and sights—for those lucky enough to experience them. The smooth surface of the water creates a dance floor for dandelion fluff. If the wind's been blowing, piles of leaves gather and slow your paddling. Once a recreational destination, way back before the interstate highway system, and recovering from decades of abuse by us humans, the Tualatin River is now a flat-water-paddlers place to go.

BY SUE MARSHALL

DESIGN + ILLUSTRATION BY ALISSA THIELE

Story Notes

by Melissa Delzio

On the following pages, you will find notes for each story in the book that will provide additional information and background to the stories submitted by the author. It is by no means a comprehensive review of the subjects broached in this book, rather it is a brief overview written with the hope that readers explore and learn more about topics of their interest.

------------------------ Page 6 ------------------------

A year or so later and the debate over the "Made in Oregon" sign (previously known as the "White Satin Sugar" sign, and the "White Stag Sportswear" sign) is still hot and heavy. The giant sign is affixed atop the White Stag Building (70 NW Couch Street), facing the Burnside Bridge. The leaping deer (an addition by the White Stag company) has become quite symbolic and residents look forward to the holidays every year when the deer's nose is lit a bright red. The sign became a historic landmark in 1978, yet has always been maintained commercially. There is still much debate about the sign, as Natalie describes. The latest word, as of March 2010, is that the sign will simply read "Portland, Oregon," although there are still groups throwing their own proposals into the mix. How about "Make in Oregon," to promote that this is a city that creates?

The debate carries on. We shall see where it lands.

------------------------ Page 7 ------------------------

The Tik Tok Drive-in was Portland's first drive-in, opening in 1938 on the corner of E Burnside and NE Sandy & NE 12th.

Here is a sample menu from its heyday:

Special Thick Creamy Malted Milk	.20
Golden Orange Whip	.15
Special Hamburger with Cheese	.20
Ham Waffle, with Butter and Syrup	.35

Not only is the restaurant now gone (it closed in 1971) but the complicated and notorious intersection that it stood on is being eliminated in favor of a more simplified system. The closing of the stretch of roadway, however, does not mean that the Tik Tok has been forgotten. In June of 2010, the Tik Tok Reunion Cruise-In took place at the old intersection, put on by Portland Foursquare Church and Road Knights Car Club. The event featured a classic car show, and music and food of the time.

I believe the Alberta Street Theater that Patsy refers to is the Alameda Theater (later named 30th Avenue Cinema, and Cine 30) located at NE 30th and Alberta, and built in 1926. At that time, it was located right on the streetcar route, the Alberta Line. The theater ceased to be a theater in 1978 when it was bought by Macedonia Church of God and then Victory Outreach Church. However, it was recently (March 2010) announced that this historic building will once again house a theater-going audience. Renamed the Alberta Rose Theatre, this venue will house 300 people and focus on acoustic musical acts from folk to classical to jazz.

------------------------ Page 8 ------------------------

Like our neighbor to the north, Portland takes extreme pride in its coffee, the independently-owned shops that serve it, and of course the hard-core micro roasters. A search on Yelp will return over 600 local coffee shops in Portland. Plenty of opportunities for all to begin their own standing Saturday coffee date.

------------------------ Page 9 ------------------------

Clinton Kelly High School of Commerce (or Commerce High School for short) is now known as Cleveland High School and is located at 3400 SE 26th Avenue. The Paramount Theater Alice describes is now called Arlene Schnitzer Concert Hall or "The Schnitz" and is home to the iconic 65ft "Portland" sign lit by theatrical lights. Like the rest of the United States, Oregon was fully involved in many aspects of the war effort during WWII.

The announcement of Japanese surrender came on August 14, 1945, the day Alice describes. In preparation for the celebration, and in fear of riots, Governor Snell of Oregon, and Brigadier General Raymond Olson, the acting Adjutant General of the Oregon Military Department, issued a proclamation closing all liquor stores in the state. They called on citizens to be "sober and patriotic," by attending church services and offering thanksgiving prayers. While victory celebrations did break out in abundance in Portland, they were mostly non-violent. An impromptu parade erupted on Broadway, fireworks crackled, horns sounded, and, as the *Oregonian* would later report, "girls kissed sailors to signify their joy at the end of the war, and particularly exuberant sailors kissed girls at random." To learn more about Portland's role in WWII visit: http://bluebook.state.or.us/cultural/history/history26.htm

STORY NOTES

---------------------- Page 10 ----------------------
Woody Guthrie was hired by the Bonneville Power Administration in 1941 to write songs for a movie they were producing called *The Columbia*. Delayed by the war, this movie was finally produced in 1949. Now it is only available on loan through the BPA library. Reserve it online at: www.bpa.gov/corporate/kr/ed/reslist

Of Woody's month-long Portland experience, Alan Lomax, American folklorist, says, "To Woody, poet of the rain-starved Dust Bowl, this mighty stream of cool, clear water, coursing through evergreen forests, verdant meadows, and high deserts was like a vision of paradise. He saw the majestic Grand Coulee Dam as the creation of the common man to harness the river for the common good – work for the jobless, power to ease household tasks, power to strengthen Uncle Sam in his fight against world fascism."

---------------------- Page 11 ----------------------
Portland has been home to many poets including William Stafford, Hazel Hall, and Walt Curtis.

William Stafford was a professor at Lewis and Clark College in 1948, left by 1955, and then returned in 1958, remaining until his death. He was named Poet Laureate of Oregon in 1975, and is the father of Kim Stafford (author of story on page 40).

Hazel Hall (1886 - 1924), referred to as the "Emily Dickinson of Oregon," had her poetry published by *Harper's Magazine*, *The New Republic*, *The Nation*, and *Yale Review*, among others. Her house in Portland is still located on NW 22nd and there is a small park erected in her honor by the Oregon Cultural Heritage Commission. The park is located on NW 22nd Place between NW Everett and W Burnside.

Walt Curtis is known for being a Beat Generation writer and poet and for writing the autobiographical *Mala Noche* (made into a movie by Gus Van Sant). Walt is a living Portland icon, painter, and host of the KBOO (community radio) poetry show "Talking Earth." Recently, Walt Curtis lost most of his belongings, writings and art in a fire at his home and studio in the Great Northwest Bookstore. There is a fund set up to help Walt get back on his feet after the fire and you can contribute at any Wells Fargo Bank to the Walt Curtis Fund.

---------------------- Page 12 ----------------------
Portland's Chinatown is located north of W Burnside between the Waterfront and Broadway. While many parts of the neighborhood are turning into higher-end shops and restaurants, there are still plenty of authentic Chinese restaurants, as described by Brian, that make the area distinct.

---------------------- Page 13 ----------------------
Many are familiar with "The Simpsons" connection to Portland with creator Matt Groening having grown up here, and graduated from Lincoln High School on SW 16th and Salmon. Portlanders take pride in knowing that many of the characters' names in the TV show are based off on Portland street names (Flanders, Quimby, Lovejoy). Less well known is the story of Homer, Matt's father. It is really the story of the beginning of Portland's creative industry; a time when Janzten Swimwear was as ubiquitous as Nike is in Portland's agency scene today.

---------------------- Page 14 ----------------------
Some may argue that St. Johns is becoming more and more decidedly hip, with new shops and restaurants investing in the area. St. Johns boasts Cathedral Park under the St. Johns Bridge (the iconic and majestic green suspension bridge), its own Jazz Festival, in addition to St. Johns Bizarre festival and parade in May.

---------------------- Page 15 ----------------------
Division Street Corral was located at SE Division and SE 171st. It was knocked down in 2007, and the land is currently under construction as the future home of D-Street Corral Condos. There are many wonderful and poignant memories of this early dance hall posted at: www.pnwbands.com/divisionstreetcorral

The New Oregon Singers was a non-profit singing group founded by Bruce Kelly in 1965. The group traveled to over 45 countries and all proceeds were donated to local charities and children's hospitals in each of the countries in which they performed. The Portland Opera is currently in its 45th season, and continues to produce ground-breaking shows. Portland Opera was one of the first to use projected English translations, and also incorporate a full offering of Broadway productions. Their 2010/2011 season begins in September 2010. You can find out more about Portland Opera at www.portlandopera.org

---------------------- Page 16 ----------------------
Oaks Bottom Wildlife Refuge is a 140-acre (160-acre by other accounts) floodplain wetland located at SE 7th Avenue and Sellwood Boulevard. The refuge winds along the north bank of the Willamette River and there are biking and hiking trails woven through it. Lying at the southernmost end of the refuge is Oaks Amusement Park, operating since 1905, and featuring a large wooden roller skating rink.

The local microbrews that Mike enjoys are a Blue Heron ale from Bridgeport Brewing, Hammerhead ale from McMenamins, and Lucky Lab stout from Lucky Labrador Brewing Company.

---------------------- Page 17 ----------------------
There are still many opportunities to take a peek into the past via Portland's various cast-iron wonders. One prominent building still standing is the Blagen Block, built in 1888, and located at 80 NW Couch Street. Organizations like the Architectural Heritage Center work to preserve Portland's rich architectural history. They regularly host walking tours, exhibits and other educational events that are open to the

STORY NOTES

public. For more information on preserving Portland's historic architecture, visit: www.visitahc.org

---------------------- Page 18 ------------------------

This twisted Portland event takes place in October every year. In 2009, over 1,000 zombies came out of hiding and gathered together in unity to walk the streets of Portland. The rules of the event state that you should stay in "zombie character" so long as it is appropriate, but should "break character" and walk normal speed while crossing intersections. These zombies are thoughtful in another way too: the event is a fundraiser for the Oregon Food Bank.

---------------------- Page 19 ------------------------

The cast-metal hogs described by Paul are two large lounging pigs resting on the sidewalk outside Nob Hill Bar & Grill on NW 23rd and NW Lovejoy.

As Paul mentioned, the Horse Project is ongoing. People are encouraged to add their own horses, or adopt a ring, which means to watch out and care for a horse currently on a ring. You can learn more and join this quirky, uniquely Portland public art project at www.horseproject.net

---------------------- Page 20 ------------------------

Like Walker, many Portlanders have fleeting memories relating to place. One Portlander, Abe Ingle, set out to record some of those memories in a project called Neighborhood Diaries. In 2009 he diligently recorded and documented people's location-based memories from several very specific neighborhoods around town. He then edited them, combined them with music, and created free interactive audio tours. Listen in at: hoodturkey.com/neighborhood-diaries

---------------------- Page 21 ------------------------

The Steel Bridge is truly a Portland workhorse. This double-lift bridge has two decks, the lower carrying pedestrian, bicycle, and railroad traffic. The upper deck carries automobile traffic and the MAX (light rail). It is possible to hear the whistle of the train, the rumble of the MAX, the buzzing of cars, the shout of a biker saying "on your left," and the grumble of a motorboat beneath you, all at the same time. The Steel Bridge marks one end of the popular three-mile jogging/walking loop that takes you down the Eastbank Esplanade all the way to the Hawthorne Bridge and then back through the westside waterfront.

---------------------- Page 22 ------------------------

As with any city and its transportation system, Portlanders have a love/hate relationship with TriMet. Folks may complain when trains are running late, the buses came too early, or the streetcar is too crowded, and yet it is because of TriMet that Portland consistently is rated one of the most accessible and sustainable cities in the country. Many TriMet travelers will have stories similar to Katy's because of the diversity of riders. From the strictly airport-bound businessman to the single mother on her way to the grocery store, to the hipster with headphones, riders are exposed to a true cross-section of the Portland population. Catch a ride at: trimet.org

---------------------- Page 23 ------------------------

Since 2001, Evolutionary Jass Band's open door band member policy often gives them a revolving cast of Portland's busiest musicians. Their steadiest lineup ended when bassist Bob Jones moved to NYC ending a core group that had played around town since 2005. While the band's shows may be criminally under-publicized, keep a keen eye peeled for posters around town or their often un-updated myspace.

Band founder, Jefry Leighton Brown, also launched Jaffe Records (jafferecords.com) which represents EJB and his own projects. Other band members have many other side projects. Jesse Munro (trumpet) performs in Gulls, Marissa Anderson (guitars) has an upcoming solo record coming out on Mississippi Records, and drummer Michael Henrickson (drums) plays/played in many bands around town (Eat Skull, Cheap Flight, JOMF).

---------------------- Page 24 ------------------------

I'm sure we can all admit that we have been tempted at some point by the Free Box. Just a casual browsing through a box, carefully placed at a neighborhood street corner by a homeowner trying to clean out the kitchen, living room or garage, as it may be. I personally have a couple of plants and a frying pan that I can attribute to this unassuming cardboard box of discovery.

This concept is taken to the next level by the Portland Free Store (www.freestoreportland.org) whose Free Box Bazaar event was first held in 2009 and is expected to occur again in 2010. It seems as though this organization is still getting off the ground, so keep your eye on them for more to come!

---------------------- Page 25 ------------------------

There are many creatives capturing, through photography, the wonder they perceive and discover in Portland. Flickr.com has an impressive system of galleries displaying images inspired by Portland posted by photographers of all levels of experience. Check out www.flickr.com/groups/pdx/ for a sample listing of groups that are dedicated to documenting the beautiful details in the Portland landscape that may go unnoticed by others.

---------------------- Page 26 ------------------------

Due to the marine west coast climate of the Pacific Northwest, Portland is rich in many varieties of flora that keep the city colorful year-round. Of course roses are the obvious example, with 550 varieties on view at the International Rose Test Garden. Portland also grows, in abundance, hydrangeas, often blue or lavender in color due to acidic soils.

Find a colorful addition to your yard at one of the many local nurseries, including Portland Nursery which has served the

STORY NOTES

community since 1907 (www.portlandnursery.com). Or, view Portland's own garden in the wild with over 1,000 species of trees and plants at Hoyt Arboretum (4000 SW Fairview Boulevard).

---------------------- Page 27 ------------------------

In addition to being heavily populated by transplants, Portland also has gained attention for its higher populations of young people aged 25-34. As of the 2000 census, these people made up 18% of the population, and my bet is that the 2010 census will show that number will have increased.

---------------------- Page 28 ------------------------

According to a map, the antipodes of Portland — that is, the geographically opposite or diametrically opposed — location on earth is, well, smack dab in the middle of the Indian Ocean. But the closest large land mass to that location would be Australia. Australians are 17 hours ahead of Portland time, so traveling back to Portland for Simon must indeed have felt like a time-traveling journey.

---------------------- Page 29 ------------------------

As of the 2000 Census, 41% of Portlanders were born in another state compared to the national rate of 27%. Want proof? Just start asking folks on any Portland street where they're from. At any rate, Portland's growth rate continues to surpass national averages. A 2008 projection estimates the population will increase from 1.3 million to 1.9 million over the next 50 years. It seems as though Portland's culture will continue to attract many more transplants like Amber.

---------------------- Page 30 ------------------------

The Lloyd Center mall was built in 1960 and named for a Californian oil company executive, Ralph B. Lloyd. As Roberta explains, the mall was open-air and originally anchored by: Meier & Frank, Lipman & Wolfe, J. C. Penney and Woolworth.

A renovation in 1991 enclosed the mall. Today the Lloyd Center mall features the department store line-up that is typical in modern American shopping landscapes. In addition, the mall of today has a movie theater and an indoor ice rink. The Lloyd Center is located at 2201 NE Lloyd Center and is accessible by the MAX light rail line.

I found very little information about the Holladay Grade School except that it was adjacent to Holladay Park (currently the park in front of Lloyd Center). The street, school and park were named for Ben Holladay, a notoriously shady character who sold his stagecoach business in California, and sought his fortune building railroads in Oregon. Instead, he overstretched his means, went bankrupt in the Panic of 1873, and died in Portland.

---------------------- Page 31 ------------------------

Located all over the city, Portland's public water fountains are free destinations for locals and tourists alike. They operate spring through fall from 6:30am to 8:00pm. As mentioned in the Story Notes entry from page 79, several fountains were designed by famous architect, Lawrence Halprin. Popular fountains for children to cool off and splash around in the summer months are the Jamison Square Fountain at NW Kearney and NW 10th, and Bill Naito Legacy Fountain at Waterfront Park (near the Burnside Bridge). Water is continuously recirculated and varies in depth and force, much to the wonderment of its visitors both young and old. You can download a Portland water fountain map from the Portland Water Bureau, or visit www.portlandwaterfountains.com for a listing.

---------------------- Page 32 ------------------------

Dots Cafe is located in the heart of the small Clinton neighborhood, at 2521 SE Clinton St. It is a Portland hipster's favorite place for late night fries, cheap drinks and velvet painting decor.

---------------------- Page 33 ------------------------

The stereotype holds that Portlanders love their tattoos. With over 110 parlors, there are plenty of opportunities for people of all backgrounds — from professional artists to lawyers to real estate agents — to make their artistic expression permanent.

Portland also has a reputation for being a more tolerant, accepting, and welcoming place for the lesbian, gay and bi-sexual community. Organizations like The Rosetown Ramblers (the Portland affiliate of the International Association of Gay Square Dance Clubs) and, more seriously, Basic Rights Oregon (a pro-active rights movement) serve and celebrate the community. The Gay Pride parade, put on annually for 40 years now by Portland Pride, occurs in June and ends at a festival at Waterfront Park. Find out more at: www.pridenw.org

---------------------- Page 34 ------------------------

While Portland celebrity Gus Van Sant, director of, among other films, *My Own Private Idaho*, *Good Will Hunting*, and *Milk* is no longer listed in the phonebook, he is still an active and respected Portland community member. In 2007 he released a movie made in Portland titled, *Paranoid Park* that features Portland's infamous Burnside Skatepark. Van Sant's next movie is *Restless*, set to debut late 2010 or early 2011.

Ariel describes Portland's Guild Theatre. Originally known as Taylor Street Theatre, it operated from 1948 until its recent closure. Located at 829 SW 9th Avenue, it is awaiting a buyer to revive this historic space.

---------------------- Page 35 ------------------------

Dustin paints a perfect picture of the type of unique experiences offered by the McMenamins Mission Theater. (More about McMenamins in Story Notes entry from page 64.) Will Oldham is an example of a multi-talented artist taking advantage of this unique opportunity. Will's latest project

STORY NOTES

is a musical release by Bonnie "Prince" Billy & The Cairo Gang called "The Wonder Show of the World."

Page 36

VooDoo Doughnut is Portland's famously unique doughnut shop. To experience it to the max, stop by right around 1am on a weekend night. That's when the line forms, and the shop is filled with interesting characters, often costumed. Most are delirious after a good night out on the town, a night that would be incomplete without one of VooDoo's delicious creations. VooDoo is located at: 22 SW 3rd Avenue.

Page 37

The First Thursday Art Walk is a favorite activity for Portlanders and visitors alike, particularly in the summer. On the first Thursday of every month, the entire Old Town/Pearl District comes alive. Galleries and shops stay open late — usually to 9pm — and host a slew of visitors sipping on (often) free wine and munching on Tillamook cheese squares. Many gallery spaces, like the Everett Station Galleries at NW 6th and NW Everett, are live/work artist spaces. There you can usually find quite a variety of artistic experiences ranging from motion/sound exhibits to clothing/jewelry displays. First Thursday Art Walk occurs all year-round, but is most popular and prominent in the summer months. In addition, from April - November, NW 13th Street between Hoyt and Kearney is closed off for a huge outdoor arts & crafts fair complete with minstrel bands and other street performers. Learn more about First Thursday and download printable walking maps at: http://padaoregon.org

Page 38

The design of the statue of Portlandia is said to be taken from the seal of Portland. The seal, adopted in 1878, has a woman in the center holding a trident in her right hand, and her left hand points to the left, almost casually, at a forest. There is a six-pointed star floating above her head, and she is looking off to the right, the opposite direction of where she is pointing. She is standing next to a river and is surrounded by items such as a cogwheel and a sledgehammer. According to the City of Portland, the female figure represents the Queen of Commerce, and the items around her represent Portland's agrarian base.

Page 39

Portland prides itself in being very neighborhood-orientated with different districts taking on their own style and flavor. There is no shortage of small neighborhood brewpubs. Don't judge a book by its cover: many unassuming locales boast a hearty selection of ales. Some notable neighborhood pubs are: Horse Brass Pub at 4534 SE Belmont Street; Tugboat Brewing Company at 711 SW Ankeny Street; or Saraveza at 1004 N Killingsworth Street.

Page 40

Kim's project is a wonderful example of a Portlander working to create wonder in small ways throughout the city. Portland's public art program is among the oldest in the nation and is largely managed by the Regional Arts & Culture Council, or RACC. Through artists residencies, grants, mural programs and more, RACC is a driving force behind employing artists and maintaining the public art library. Some notable public art pieces are: Da Tung & Xi'an Bao Bao (aka the funky elephant at NW 9th Avenue and W Burnside Street); the Portlandia statue (see Story Notes entry from page 38); and one of the most recent additions, People's Bike Library of Portland (W Burnside Street & SW 13th Avenue).

Download a walking map of all Portland's notable public art displays at: racc.org

Page 41

Sledgehammer is held in Portland every fall, but can be found online every day of the year at sledgehammercontest.com and on Facebook and Twitter. Also join Indigo Editing & Publications, the contest host, for other events throughout the year, including 36-minute Mini Sledgehammers every second Tuesday at Blackbird Wine Shop (http://blackbirdwine.com) in NE Portland.

Page 42

Rachel's mom isn't the only Karen making noise on the Portland scooter scene. Karen Giezyng — aka Kickstart Karen — is a Portland scooter-rider and zinester, publisher of *Bumpstart*, the Pacific NW Scooter Zine. Learn more about her Portland scooter adventures at: www.kickstartkaren.blogspot.com

More about the scooter scene in Portland in Story Notes entry from page 51.

Page 43

That's right, dodgeball. Adult Portlanders have been enjoying this and other alternative sports long before Hollywood made them popular. Organizations like Recess Time have created over 4,000 co-ed teams around the sports of kickball, dodgeball, bowling, ping pong, and mushball. While these leagues have the promise of combining the magic of childhood play with the lure of an alcoholic after-party, I can speak from experience that dodgeball competitions are not all fun and games. Matches can get pretty intense when adults stand within 20ft of each other and hurl large, bright red balls (yes they cause bruising). But, glory and excitement can be revived by the successful sinking of one single "Scotty Shot" (ball made into the opposing side's basketball hoop).

Join or sign up your team at: recesstimesports.com

Page 44

The Ladd Carriage House was built in 1883 by William Sargent Ladd, Portland's fifth mayor. The house was moved in 2007 to a temporary location in a church parking lot, while the block was redeveloped to make way for a new condo complex and church expansion. Then, the house was care-

STORY NOTES

fully moved back to its original location in 2008. All of this is thanks to the organization Friends of Ladd Carriage House and their many supporters. So what is the status of the house now? Well, it is for sale. Fully renovated, beautiful and comfortable in its new/old landscape, the property could be yours for a cool $1,950,000. Possible home of Our Portland Story? Follow the project at: www.laddcarriagehouse.org

---------------------- Page 45 ----------------------
Forest Park, one of the largest urban forest reserves, stretches for over eight miles. More than 112 bird and 62 mammal species call it home. It boasts miles of trails that interconnect and cut through the park, the longest of which, the Wildwood, runs 27 miles. Holman Meadow can be found at the end of NW Raleigh Street where it meets NW Aspen. Learn about Forest Park at: http://forestparkconservancy.org

---------------------- Page 46 ----------------------
Portland has a rich and vibrant history of streetcar use and many of its roads are littered with old rails barely peeking through the asphalt. Now, as Portland again seeks to expand its streetcar lines, the Portland Vintage Trolley organization is dedicated to preserving that history. Find out more at: http://vintagetrolleys.com

Portlander Abigail Duniway was the American West's leading women's advocate. In 1871, she began publishing a weekly newspaper, *The New Northwest*, supporting human rights, education and suffrage. Her efforts paid off and she was the first woman to register to vote in Multnomah County.

---------------------- Page 47 ----------------------
The Western Trillium in Oregon, and other species of the spring ephemeral perennials, are native to North America. Michael is correct in his claim that picking a trillium causes serious injury to the plant for years, so much so that in Michigan, Minnesota, and parts of the Canadian province of Ontario, it is actually illegal to pick the flower. The large white trillium is the official wildflower of Ohio and is the emblem for Ontario.

---------------------- Page 48 ----------------------
Steve's friend, Bill, describes Klamath Falls, a city in Southern Oregon where he had an Appaloosa, a horse breed that has been traced back to the Native Americans of the Pacific Northwest.

Steve clearly appreciates these regular visits from Bill. Reading this strangely soothing story, and thanks to Steve's way with words, one can see the two of them — one younger, one older — sitting amongst "the finest in Chinese plastic and gearation," which Bill puts to shame with his stories and insights.

---------------------- Page 49 ----------------------
The West Hills are full of hidden staircases that lead you from the top of the Vista Bridge, with its panoramic views of the city, down through mossy enclaves and wind you between the million dollar homes only to spit you out in the Goose Hollow neighborhood.

Portland's Weather Machine resides in Pioneer Square atop a metal column, 33 feet tall. It was constructed in 1988 and every day at noon it will announce the next day's weather with a short trumpet introduction. The silver orb on top of the column will open up and out will emerge a golden burst (meaning sunshine), a blue heron (meaning overcast), or a dragon (meaning storm). Lights on the side flash and indicate temperature.

---------------------- Page 50 ----------------------
Sauvie Island is bordered by the Columbia River to the north, the Willamette River to south, and the Multnomah Channel to the west. On the island, Portlanders escaping the city can explore the nature trails, lounge on the sandy beaches, shop at a farmer's market, or participate in one of the many farms' U-pick programs.

In October, as Scott describes, the island really comes alive with pumpkin patches, hay rides, corn mazes (haunted at night), petting zoos, and plenty of hot kettle corn.

---------------------- Page 51 ----------------------
A recent survey of 1,000 motorcycle and scooter owners conducted by the City of Portland showed that over 56% of respondents belong to a motorcycle or scooter organization. With over 20,000 riders in Multnomah County alone, there are many active communities out there uniting scooter riders. To learn more about the Twist N Play Scooter Club, visit www.twistnplay.com.

---------------------- Page 52 ----------------------
Perhaps Portland's independent spirit is rooted in its pioneer history starting with the explorers Lewis & Clark and the early settlers arriving in their Conestoga wagons. Regardless, Portland has since taken the lead in many national firsts. Portland was the first city in the nation to hire a policewoman in 1908 and in 2008, Portland elected Sam Adams, the first openly gay mayor of a top 30 U.S. city. In 1993, Portland became the first U.S. city to adopt a Global Warming Action Plan. And, in 2001, was also the first to develop this nation's most modern streetcar system. Is it a coincidence that Portland's NBA sports team is named the TrainBlazers? One could argue not.

---------------------- Page 53 ----------------------
According to a 2009 report, Portland has one of the highest homeless populations in the nation. Central City Concern, Julia West House, and p:ear are a few of the many organizations offering programs to provide services to this population in Portland.

CJ is different from so many other homeless in that he remains an active member of the Portland scene/culture.

STORY NOTES

Write About Portland is a non-profit organization dedicated to transforming lives through writing (writearound.org). Fright Town is an annual Haunted House held at the Rose Quarter every October.

---------------------- Page 54 ------------------------

Lake Oswego (pronounced Os_wee_go) is a southern suburb of Portland. The Children's Garden can be found at 125 Rosemont Road (just off Stafford Road). Community Gardens in Portland, run by Portland Parks and Recreation, also have programming for children including free summer gardening classes.

---------------------- Page 55 ------------------------

Mount Tabor is an extinct volcano dotting Portland's eastside landscape. This ancient mountain with its park spaces and walking trails is now a haven for eastside dog-walkers, park-goers, joggers, and lovebirds. The volcanic soil makes for fertile ground, to the great joy of gardeners. Urban farming has become a way of life for many Portlanders, where raised vegetable beds have replaced the iconic front lawn. With the recent surge in popularity, chickens are now a common sight in Portland backyards. In fact, Portland now has the highest urban chicken population per capita in the country, and the city allows residents to keep up to three chickens without needing a permit.

---------------------- Page 56 ------------------------

Most days in Portland, the closest you can come to honoring "the King" is by visiting the famous 24-hour Church of Elvis window display on 408 NW Couch. However, Dan's Elvis experience came in the form of one of Portland's many regular street performers. In addition to Elvis, there is the man who rides around in a van with a wooden sculptured facade, blasting a variety of oldies hits. There is the gentleman who wears a white suit, dons Mickey Mouse ears and plays a trumpet, sometimes to the pre-Blazer game crowd as they're walking to the game, or maybe to drivers who commute over the Hawthorne Bridge. These performers are part of the fabric that enlivens the streets, catches you off-guard, and makes you smile.

---------------------- Page 57 ------------------------

Saturday/Sunday morning (11am) brunch in Portland is a must after a long night of microbrew and VooDoo Doughnut consumption. Many of the popular places will have loyal customers waiting patiently on the sidewalk for a table, sipping coffee while they wait (often from the establishment's unique mugs). Brunch spots range from the casual outdoor patio/garden experience of Tin Shed (1438 NE Alberta Street) to the southern comfort of Screen Door (2337 E Burnside) to the more established, historically prominent Besaw's (2301 NW Savier Street). The eclectically decorated Stepping Stone that Chris describes is located at 2390 NW Quimby Street.

---------------------- Page 58 ------------------------

As evidenced by this story, Portland is very supportive of various forms of new performance art, even ones that spoof other performative art. Jodi's creation of Cat-Based Art is an homage to PICA's (Portland Institute for Contemporary Art) Time-Based Art. Catch up with the Cattitude team at: www.myspace.com/cattitudedanceensemble

---------------------- Page 59 ------------------------

The Time-Based Art (TBA) Festival is put on by Portland Institute for Contemporary Art (PICA). It takes place every year in September and draws talent from across the globe for a 10-day festival of contemporary performance, dance, music, new media, and visual arts projects. Events are held all over town and range in price, and some are even free.

---------------------- Page 60 ------------------------

You may have a hard time finding folks who agree with Eloise's love of the weather in the middle of a rainy winter, but it's true that Portland's weather is full of surprises. It seems like there is always a glorious, sunny, beautifully warm day in February that comes around just to tease and provide hope for spring's arrival.

---------------------- Page 61 ------------------------

Painting "en plein air" is a French phrase describing the act of painting outdoors. It was popularized by the French (Monet and friends) in the 1870s with the advent of paint in tubes and box easels. In Portland, painting en plein air is still popular amongst many artists. If you are seeking to embark on a painting adventure, The Portland Plein Air Painters meet twice a week to plot and plan their next journey. You can join them at: portlandpleinairandstudiopainters.blogspot.com

---------------------- Page 62 ------------------------

Enthusiasts claim Portland as the fabric store capital of the world, and with stores like Mill End Store (9701 SE McLoughlin Boulevard) and Fabric Depot (700 SE 122nd Avenue), it is hard to argue. Portland has its roots in wool with the Thomas Kay Woolen Mill, founded in 1889 by Thomas L. Kay in Salem. Later, his son-in-law, C.P. Bishop, would move the family business to Pendleton, Oregon, and the company was thus renamed, Pendleton Woolen Mills. The Oregon Worsted Company (now Mill End Store) was created to fill the need for soldiers' uniforms during WWI, and was started by C.P.'s son, Roy Bishop. Today the Pendleton company is still run by descendents of the Bishop family.

The now signature Pendleton shirt, with its bright plaid, was popularized by a singing group known as the Pendletones, until they later decided on a new name. You might recognize them better as The Beach Boys.

---------------------- Page 63 ------------------------

The Brasserie Montmartre is now no longer defunct! It is a historic Portland restaurant reminiscent of a fine Parisian eatery, and is located at 626 SW Park Avenue.

STORY NOTES

The Cornelius Hotel, home to the original p:ear location, was once of the most unique and elegant hotels in Portland when it opened in 1908. Over time, it gained new reputations, such as its 1960s and 1970s function as a bathhouse for gays. The future of the now abandoned building is uncertain as plans for the building's rebirth as the Alder Park Hotel are up in the air.

Johnny Sole (shoe store) and Rich's Cigar Shop have moved to new locations at 815 SW Alder Street and 820 SW Alder Street, respectively.

Joy, Pippa and Beth's creation, p:ear, is now a leading non-profit, reaching out to Portland's homeless street youth through creative mentorship. Be sure to stop by their monthly art opening on First Thursday (see Story Notes entry from page 37) to see the youths' artwork and meet the ladies. p:ear is located at NW 6th and Flanders.

Page 64

The well-known pink-house restaurant that Chris describes is a building located at 938 N Cook Street. The building used to house Lovely Hula Hands, but currently is home to The Liberty Glass, a bar and restaurant. There are many old churches, schools and other such buildings of a different era that have since been converted into new multi-use spaces such as movie theaters, bars, and restaurants. Many of these buildings, such as The Kennedy School (5736 NE 33rd Avenue) and Chapel Pub (430 N Killingsworth Street) are run by McMenamins, a unique Northwest chain that restores and embellishes with art the historic buildings they take over. Find out more about McMenamins at: www.mcmenamins.com

Page 65

It has been well over a year now, and there is still no sign yet of "Hung Far Low's" re-emergence. The sign, when it was proudly displayed, marked the facade of what was the second oldest restaurant in Chinatown, first established in 1929.

The original restaurant has since moved to 2410 SE 82nd Avenue. Although the restaurant has moved on, there is an organization dedicated to raising money to restore the sign and return it to its Chinatown home. You may join their cause at: www.reerecthungfarlow.com

Page 66

Skaters for Portland Skateparks is an organization motivated by a mission to create a comprehensive system of world-class public skateparks. An early step towards accomplishing this goal was the plan to work with city councils to create a nineteen-park system. Next up is securing an official indoor facility for the skating population during the rainy months. One of the most popular skate facilities is Burnside, located under the Burnside Bridge on the eastside. This location was built by skateboarders and only later approved by the City. Check out skateportland.org for more details.

Page 67

In Portland the average rainfall is 37.5 inches. The wettest months of the year are: November, December and January, each with slightly over five inches. Matt Zaffino is the Chief Meteorologist for KGW, one of Portland's numerous television stations.

Page 68

When it snows in Portland, usually once or twice a year, all hell breaks loose. With limited means to manage snow-accumulated streets, the city effectively shuts down. Traffic grinds to a halt as snow-adverse drivers crawl along the foreign landscape. At the same time, the unusual occurrence of snow brings out a certain giddiness in Portland kids and adults alike. Lacking true snow gear (sleds and apparel), Portlanders often find creative ways to have fun. See this firsthand by going to youtube.com and searching for: "Couch on a mission Portland."

Page 69

Citybikes is a worker-owned co-op located, for sales, at 734 SE Ankeny and for service at 1914 SE Ankeny. The sticker "Bicycles Allowed Full Lane" is intended to promote awareness of Oregon law 814.430 which states that bike riders in Oregon are allowed full use of lane when it is necessary to avoid surface hazards or other conditions that make it unsafe to ride on the right-hand side of the road.

Page 70

Yes, this is Beervana. As you probably already know, Portland, with 38 breweries, has more of these establishments than any other city in the world. Portland is also host to the best-attended beer festival in the nation, the Oregon Brewers Festival, hosting 50,000 people every year on the Waterfront in the last weekend of July. Beer is also a big economic driver in the state, employing 4,700 full-time and part-time employees. Find out more at the Oregon Brewer's Guild (oregonbeer.org) or join the crowd at the Oregon Brew Fest (www.oregonbrewfest.com).

Page 71

Albina Press has two locations, one on Hawthorne (5012 SE Hawthorne Boulevard) and one on Albina (4637 N Albina Avenue). They serve Stumptown coffee, purchased from the locally owned coffee shop and roaster of the same name. Part of what makes Stumptown coffee a Portland favorite is that the company promotes direct trade, offers many organic options and serves varietals from all over the world. While they have expanded their operation to New York and Amsterdam, you can still chat with local experts during the cupping sessions, held daily at 11am and 3pm at Stumptown Annex (3352 SE Belmont Street).

Page 72

The 57 line Dave refers to is TriMet's bus line going from Portland to Forest Grove and vice versa. Just 24 miles away, Forest Grove is surrounded by rich farmland and wineries.

STORY NOTES

While rural in setting, as Dave mentioned, it is still just a bus ride away from the bustling city of Portland.

---------------------- Page 73 -------------------------

Powell's Books (1005 W Burnside Street) is the largest used and new bookstore in the world, and a Mecca for Portlanders and visitors alike. In Powell's, books are sorted by subject matter into different rooms represented by colors. Looking for fiction? The Blue Room is your place — note the extensive local zine selection. Like the arts and music? Head to the Pearl Room, and be sure to check out the latest exhibit in the art gallery also on this floor. Thirsty? Then head for World Cup coffee in the Yellow Room — don't step on any book-involved Trekkies on your way through the sci-fi section. Lost? There is even a map for that.

---------------------- Page 74 -------------------------

Since the writing of this story, the Portland Classical Chinese Garden has changed its name to Lan Su Chinese Garden to reflect its relationship with its sister city, Suzhou, in China. "Lan" stands for Portland; "Su," for Suzhou. Lan Su is located at 239 NW Everett Street, and the cost of admission ranges from $6.50 to $8.50. When you visit, be sure to come hungry so you can stimulate your tastebuds at Lan Su's Teahouse while simultaneously soaking in the peacefulness of the garden. The Teahouse has a full menu of teas and small plates including such delicious delicacies as turnip cakes and steamed buns.

---------------------- Page 75 -------------------------

It is no secret that Ben and Laura's desire to live a more sustainable life is shared by many Portlanders. Both Portland and the state of Oregon offer financial incentives that cover 80% of solar panel installation costs for homeowners (more for businesses), making Oregon incentives some of the best in the nation. The Metro Regional Government offers wide resources on recycling and waste prevention, composting, bike routes, and food donation (www.oregonmetro.gov).

Portland's sustainability commitment goes well beyond that, and there is a plethora of organizations serving various niches. Some of these organizations are: Slow Food Portland (www.slowfoodportland.com), Ecotrust (www.ecotrust.org), and the Portland Sustainability Institute (www.pdxinstitute.org). The efforts of many different organizations will culminate in the Oregon Sustainability Center, a $120 million dollar project that strives to be a center for innovation, discussion, and green business, while positioning Portland as a global leader in green building, clean technology, and environmental stewardship. Support the effort at: oregonsustainabilitycenter.org

---------------------- Page 76 -------------------------

Tryon Creek is an Oregon State Park in the Southwestern part of Portland between Boones Ferry Road and Terwilliger Boulevard. Tryon Creek houses a nature center and includes hiking, biking, and horse trails. The Tryon River, running throughout the watershed, contains steelhead trout and coho salmon. Every year in April the organization, Friends of Tryon Creek, hosts the Trillium Festival with guided hikes, activities for kids, and crafts from local vendors. Learn more about Friends of Tryon Creek at www.tryonfriends.org

---------------------- Page 77 -------------------------

Lone Fir Cemetery is located at SE 26th Avenue and SE Stark. It hosted its first resident in 1846, and is Portland's oldest cemetery. In addition to housing a large plot of Chinese immigrants — upon which the county built a structure only later to remove it — the cemetery also contains a large plot of "inmates" from the Oregon Hospital for the Insane. The group Friends of Lone Fir and Metro are still working to right the wrongs of the treatment of the graves and erect a memorial in the Block 14 corner of the property to honor these early immigrants and pioneers.

Many headstone names will be familiar as they indicate the final resting spots of famous Portlanders from the past for whom many bridges, streets, or parks are now named. There you will find Hawthorne, Northrup, Thurman, Banfield, Sellwood, Dekum and Lovejoy.

---------------------- Page 78 -------------------------

For more on Forest Park see Story Notes entry from page 45, and for Voodoo Doughnuts see entry from page 36. The International Rose Test Garden is certainly one of the most strongly scented of all Portland locations. While directions to reach the garden by car are complicated, you can park at the base of Washington Park (at SW Vista Avenue and Park Place) and walk up through the park, following signs to the gardens. The Rose Test Garden is at its best when the roses are in full bloom in summer. Salmon Street Springs Fountain marks the entry to Waterfront Park from Downtown at SW Salmon Street and Naito. It is often populated by partially clothed, delighted, and thoroughly soaked children as well as a few adults who have unleashed their inner child and splashed through the chlorine-infused fountain waters.

Music Millennium is a Portland music-lover's treasure. Its original location, at NE 32nd and E Burnside still exists (although their NW 23rd location has shut down). It is the Powell's of music, with its extensive collection of old and new records and cassettes sharing shelf space with cds. Hunting through the many collections is part of the fun as you wind your way up and down this old brick building's rickety staircase and through multi-leveled floors, exploring the living artifacts of musical eras past and present.

---------------------- Page 79 -------------------------

Lawrence Halprin was one of the most prominent American landscape architects of his time. He was born in Brooklyn, NY, and studied in Wisconsin, where his love of architecture was influenced by the great Frank Lloyd Wright. While he spent much of his professional career in San Francisco, Halprin and his design team helped create several of the green spaces and fountains most popular in Portland. Pettygrove

STORY NOTES

Park is located at SW 1st and SW Market; Ira's Fountain is located across from Keller Auditorium at 222 SW Clay Street; and Lovejoy Fountain is located at SW Hall and SW 3rd.

For more on Portland's fountains, see Story Notes entry from page 31.

---------------------- **Page 80** ------------------------

While there are no statistics I know of to support this, it sure does seem as though Portland has a high population of highly-educated wait staff. With the downturn of the economy, many find that jobs in their chosen career path are few and far between. However, working a restaurant job in Oregon is a better path for employment here than in other states, because Oregon requires that even tipped employees get paid the full minimum wage, in addition to their tips. This is opposed to the policy in 47 other states which allows employers to pay tipped employees less.

---------------------- **Page 81** ------------------------

Bridgetown is yet another of Portland's monikers. There are 11 bridges that span the great Willamette River that cuts Portland into east and west. The beautiful and multi-functional Hawthorne Bridge is the oldest, built in 1910. It used to lead to Asylum Street in SE Portland, where you could find the Oregon Hospital for the Insane run by a Dr. Hawthorne. However, when the hospital moved to Salem, the street was renamed Hawthorne.

---------------------- **Page 82** ------------------------

The Tualatin River Keepers (TRK) is a non-profit dedicated to protecting and restoring the habitat that Sue loves. TRK offers paddling trips, nature education and advocacy. Their volunteers work with government and local businesses to prevent urban stormwater pollution and protect water quality. The TRK are working towards their goal of creating a Tualatin River Water Trail by developing a public launch site every five miles along the river. You can donate to the cause, or learn more at www.tualatinriverkeepers.org

Your Story

Submit your story for the next book online at www.OurPortlandStory.com

_____
_____
_____
_____
_____
_____
_____
_____
_____
_____
_____
_____

Designer Credits

Designers are listed alphabetically by last name.

The designers listed here graciously donated their time to bring the authors' stories to life on the page. Please consider one of the designers from this list when looking for a partner for your next creative project.

Joe Aimonetti..*page 18*

Julie Almquist ....*page 44*
Almquist Productions
www.AlmquistProductions.com
Julie@AlmquistProductions.com
503.774.0065
Almquist Productions has successfully been in business for ten years. Working closely with her clients, Julie takes responsibility for the entire project, from concept through production, to ensure top quality products, delivered on time and within budget.

Elizabeth Avakian ....*page 52*
www.elizabethavakian.com
elizabethavakian@gmail.com
Elizabeth Avakian is a graphic designer passionate about logo/brand identity, page layout and print design. She moved from Arkansas to Portland in 2004. Elizabeth is inspired in her art and life by the music she loves.

Alice Baldwin.........................*page 37*
alicebaldwin.com
alicebaldwin@gmail.com

Scott Ballard...........................*page 39*
www.scottballardfilms.com
www.myyearinbeer.blogspot.com
Scott Ballard is a screen-printer and letterpress artist. His work is featured at www.twoguitars.etsy.com

Susan Bard ....*page 16*
susanbarddesign.com
sbard@easystreet.net
From business systems and collateral, books and catalogs to illustration, animation, motion graphics and DVD authoring, we provide professional design services. Reliable, reasonable and courteous. Gold award recipient 2010 PubWest Book Design. Silver award recipient 2009 IAPHC Book Design.

Jessie Bazata..........................*page 33*
Art Director
www.mywondereyes.com
631.926.1153
My days are filled with design, illustration and craft at the Curiosity Group. My nights are dedicated to Sweet Street Gals. I enjoy gardening, baking anything with puff pastry, and I drive a '74 Maverick the color of an unripe banana.

Crystal Beasley......................*page 25*
skinnywhitegirl.com
twitter.com/skinny
FPO IA CSS ESP PDX TMI   NSFW. Projects include @iconrainbow @pieLabPDX @sxswcrush @futuregames

Laura Sue Bentz ....*page 75*
laurasue.com
laura@laurasue.com
706.963.0851
I'm all about sustainability, and I'm all about design. So I combined two big passions into one little business: Laura Sue Design. From the ground up, my design solutions are developed ecologically — all created with love, all carbon neutral.

Rachel Beyer ....*page 78*
www.rachelbeyer.com
www.campsmartypants.com
rachelbeyer@gmail.com
Rachel is an artist and designer living in NE Portland. She received her BFA in graphic design in 2007 and has worked for many design companies in both the Seattle and Portland areas. She loves sewing, tie-dye, illustration, and crafts.

Simon Black ....*page 57*
moterepublic.com
simon@moterepublic.com
Simon is a graphic designer specializing in print and online media. He has ten years' experience in the creative industry, including roles with renowned advertising and design agencies. Simon's clients include mom and pop businesses, international non-profits, and world-leading brands.

DESIGNER CREDITS

Gerry Blakney .... pages 21, 61
Haf tohn design
www.designlocally.com
Gerry Blakney is a Portland designer specializing in print and web design.

Jacqueline Kari Bos .... pages 11, 69
www.jacquelinekari.com
bos.jacqueline@gmail.com
I am a Portland-based illustrator. Among other things I enjoy magic, myths, minty tea and wandering about my neighborhood.

Precious Bugarin .... page 40
preciousbugarin.com
Precious Bugarin Design specializes in bespoke invitations, timeless brands, and fine ephemera. Find them online at preciousbugarin.com

Kristin Casaletto .... page 77
casalettodesign.com
kristin@casalettodesign.com
417.234.5064
Kristin Casaletto is a Portland-based graphic designer, illustrator, and artist. She has worked on a variety of creative projects from wine labels and websites to wooden signs. Currently a freelancer, Kristin is regularly on the lookout for her next creative challenge.

Jay Cech .... page 15
www.jaycech.com
jaycechdesign@gmail.com
Cech Design is an independent studio in Portland, Oregon, with specialities in branding, promotional design, apparel graphic design and creative concepting. Partnering with clients from around the world as well as around the block, we achieve beautiful and efficient communication.

Jessica Chu .... page 65
www.Jessica-Chu.com
contact@Jessica-Chu.com
Grew up in the beautiful Northwest. Originally from Taiwan, Jessica graduated from the Art Institute of Portland in 2008. She is passionate about graphic design, and "Simplicity is the Standard for Beauty" is her design philosophy.

Megan Clark .... pages 9, 76
www.studiompdx.com
www.studiompdx.blogspot.com
megan@studiompdx.com
Since its onset in 2005, StudioM has become known for communication design, web design, art direction, marketing strategy and branding. Megan's clients range from boutiques and cafés to iPhone application developers and private eyes and are located across the country.

Jen Cogliantry .... page 60
www.jencogliantry.com
jen@jencogliantry.com
917.687.0160
Jen Cogliantry is a graphic designer based in Portland, OR. A transplant from New York City in 2009, her recent clients include AIA Oregon, Simon & Schuster, and Stewart, Tabori & Chang. When she is not working she can be found wandering through the Pacific Northwest with her family in their vintage camper, The Continental Crawler.

Drew Cone .... page 59
www.theurbancabin.com
drew@theurbancabin.com
My work is an ever-evolving compilation of the world around me. Things that inspire my work include the outdoors, textures, and the unique individuals I interact with everyday.

Gabrielle Drinard .... page 48
www.gabrielledrinard.com
415.722.2762
gd@gabrielledrinard.com
Gabrielle Drinard is a fine artist who arrived at design by traveling first through illustration, commercial photography, and the web. Her design is a culmination of all her interests and tends to be touched by her personality. She enjoys sports and dance.

Yvonne Perez Emerson, Cre8tivegirl .... pages 13, 54
cre8tivegirl.com
yvonne@cre8tivegirl.com
503.703.6408
Yvonne is a freelance designer/artist and an award winning design director with 15+ years' experience in print and online design. You can find her work at Cre8tivegirl.com

DESIGNER CREDITS

Lindsey C. Frei .... *page 80*
ploomstudios.com
lindseyfrei@ploomstudios.com
Visual problem solver, designer, art director, collector of hobbies and forever a student of life.

Sean Garrison.......................... *page 7*
www.seangarrison.com
971-285-5881
Sean is an illustrator, a designer, and an entrepreneur. His favorite things about Portland include the pop scene, like-minded individuals, and QFC.

Krissy Gilhooly .... *page 45*
www.potassiumdesign.com
krissy@potassiumdesign.com
Krissy's fascination with Portland started the day she moved here in 2001. Since then, she has immersed herself in the local design and music communities. Yet, her freelance experience extends beyond CD packaging to include branding, collateral, and wedding packages.

Ginkgo Synthesis.................... *page 8*
www.ginkgosynthesis.com
503.347.7195
Ginkgo Synthesis focuses on telling the stories of our clients through a mixed media mash-up of design, illustration, and animation. Portland's special brand of insanity is a constant source of inspiration for us, and we proudly call it home.

Kathleen Grebe ....*page 47*

Marisa D. Green............. *pages 10, 62*
studio danae
www.studiodanae.com
marisadanae@gmail.com
Marisa is an illustrator and graphic designer living in Portland, Oregon. She loves to travel, write, and document every day in photos. Her work is inspired by stories, colors, and patterns that cover a broad spectrum from heritage to humor.

Brittany K. Hanson............... *page 36*
www.brittanyishanson.com
brittanyishanson@gmail.com
Portland is amazing, it's everything you want it to be. It's wonderful to be an artist involved in this project, documenting these writers' personal experiences. Design+Portland =<3

Rosy Harris .... *page 43*
www.rosyharris.com
I've immersed my life and career in sports, marketing and design. I work as a full-time designer in the Marketing Department for a sports company in Portland, and I also manage my own company, FUEL Design Studios. Graphic design, web design and development, illustration and interior design are all areas that encompass my design work.

Stuart Haury .... *pages 46, 70*
www.stuarthaury.com
stuhaury@gmail.com
Stuart Haury is a visual communicator now living and working in Seattle, Washington. He enjoys design, photography, video, music, exploring, and looks forward to working with you and pushing the boundaries of print and multimedia design.

heaum, Inc..............................*page 79*
www.heaumstudio.com
hc@heaumstudio.com
heaum is owned by freelance designer Heather Carleton. Her clients range from small businesses to large national organizations (both for-profit and non-profit). She specializes in branding and identity work.

Aimee Heigold .... *page 68*
www.etsy.com/shop/aheigo
heigolda@hotmail.com
The need to create is one thing in my life that has never let me go and I'm very glad it's held on. Portland is a wonderful source of inspiration, motivation and unexpected outcomes.

Lisa Holmes .... *pages 38, 81*
www.yulanstudio.com
lholmes@yulanstudio.com
Lisa Holmes, co-founder and art director of Yulan Studio, relished the opportunity this book provided to work in photo collage — a passion carried throughout her career as a graphic designer specializing in web and interactive work.

Carrie Hoover.......................... *page 71*
www.destructokitty.com
destructokitty@me.com
Carrie is a designer, illustrator and all around creative lady. Her whimsical style for building this page was inspired by the handmade aesthetic that is so very Portland. All the materials used in this illustration are recyclable.

DESIGNER CREDITS

Martha Koenig .... page 26
marthakoenig.com
m@marthakoenig.com
Martha has been creating materials in both on-and offline worlds for the past eight years. Besides her Art Director role, she's also a committee member of AIGA Portland's sustainability team. She nerds out on letterpress novelties and epic Northwest hikes.

Rochelle Koivunen .... page 53
www.rorotoyou.com
rochelle.koivunen@gmail.com
Rochelle makes images and objects that reflect her connection with All That Is. That includes you, Rainbow Warrior.

Briar Levit .... page 64
www.briarmade.com
hello@briarmade.com
Briar Levit is a print designer who has recently made Portland her home. In addition to designing primarily for the nonprofit sector, Levit teaches at Portland State University and, in any spare time, works on her Unseen walking book series.

Jessie May Li .... page 32
www.coroflot.com/jessie
jessiemli@gmail.com
A native Portlander, Jessie enjoys collecting Stumptown vignettes and is partial to typography and the printed form. She draws inspiration from her background in art history and visual communication, admiring the works of Sargent, Ruscha, and Tschichold, to name a few.

Quentin Lueninghoener .... page 30

Beth Marquis (Perlas) .... page 67
bperlas@gmail.com
elizabethmarquis.carbonmade.com
Art and I are like best friends, like salt and pepper, or socks.

Tim May .... page 22
freshbeast.com
tim@freshbeast.com
I am a Ritalin child of the 80s. I wish I still had some — the pills were small and easy to swallow. I painted, took pictures from my car and scrawled animals with my Wacom tablet to make my contribution.

Molly McClurg .... page 27
mollymcclurg.com
mollymcclurg@yahoo.com
My work and me in 40 words (including these words). There is no one thing in the world I can spend my life doing. So I design, as an excuse to try everything and to communicate my experience while trying.

Krista Messer .... page 29
kristamesser.com
kristamesser@gmail.com
Krista Messer grew up in the sticks of Idaho Falls, ID, where she spent most summer days daydreaming in lava rocks with many cats and having frightening thoughts about bears. She now resides in Portland, OR, with her family, and is a recent graduate of PSU in printmaking and design.

Deanna Michaelson .... page 24
youvegottodosomething@gmail.com
Deanna Michaelson cranks out good design for People's Food Co-op in Southeast Portland. She has a passion for anything handmade, especially tools and food. Her Portland Story would feature lots of coffee, bike rides, house shows, collective meetings and vegan brunch.

Matt Morasky .... page 12
Citizengraphics.com
matt@citizengraphics.com
Matt Morasky has practiced design in Portland for nearly a decade. His work (and life) is fueled by the city's three trademark fluids: coffee, beer and rain.

Alicia Nagel .... page 56
www.alicianagel.com
Alicia Nagel Creative was established with the mission of creating authentic, relevant and memorable brands and providing complete graphic design services. Deliverables include: Logo, Business Card and Stationery, website, Printed and Online Marketing Materials, Branding and Marketing Strategy.

Raymond G. Perez .... page 17
www.aqueadesign.com
ray@aqueadesign.com
Good design is when form meets function. Raymond Perez, a classically trained graphic designer and illustrator, strives to create harmony in his design of websites and print materials. Aquea Design is his award-winning creative agency.

DESIGNER CREDITS

Andrew Petrie......................*page 35*
www.purple-neon.com
andrew@purple-neon.com
Andrew is a graphic designer and web developer who lives and works in Southeast Portland. His digital collages draw inspiration from the organized chaos found in music and nature.

Whitney Phu......................... *page 28*
www.whitneyphu.com
wp@whitneyphu.com
I'm a graphic designer located in Portland with a passion for packaging, color, and texture. When I'm not in front of a computer, you can find me out hiking or painting in my studio.

Geoff Pratt..............................*page 72*
www.flickr.com/photos/geoffreydesign
I used to have anxious dreams about not being able to find Waldo in Where's Waldo. I think most things I make and obsess over have that same base-level existential crisis within; searching for a Waldo that may or may not be found. Check out my stuffs, y'all!

Angela Reat............................. *page 63*
Imprint Design
http://angreat.jimdo.com
415.374.9441
angreat@yahoo.com
With over 15 years of experience working with clients such as the U.N. in Rome, Disney, and the University of California San Francisco (UCSF publications), Angela currently specializes in identity and branding for the food, beverage and hospitality industries both nationally and abroad.

Matthew Ryf...........................*page 41*
503.267.9291
mryf@comcast.net
My work is my craft. Approaching and solving problems of communication, translating verbal concepts into visual imagery, and practicing an unwavering discipline for detail-oriented work my clients value.

Emily Sapp................................*page 6*
Kitten Design
kittendesign.com
At Kitten Design, we focus heavily on concept development. No matter the medium, clarifying the message and creating a strong visual identity leads to a finished product that connects our clients to their customers in a meaningful way.

Ryan Schroeder .... *page 34*
artisticpropaganda.com
twitter: @pdxschroeder
Just another graphic designer in the best city in the world.

Troy Stange............................. *page 51*
www.pdxdesignlab.com
troy@pdxdesignlab.com
Creative design and branding.

Alissa Thiele........................... *page 82*
www.atealeaf.me
alissa.thiele@atealeaf.me
Combine one part sweet Midwestern drawl, one part savvy designer, one part hard-core crafter, with a dash of Portland, Oregon's hip independent spirit and you get mixed media artist, Alissa Thiele.

Corey Thompson........... *pages 50, 58*
www.thisiscoreythompson.com
www.shapesofsweetness.com
hello@thisiscoreythompson.com
I make illustrations and design things. Inspired by rad dudes, tasty treats, and anything deemed bad by everyone else, I will always be makin' things. I love the Blazers, PBR, and Portland. E-mails are dope so don't be afraid to send me one.

Kat Topaz...................................*page 19*
topazdesign.com
Topaz has launched dozens of redesigns, including the San Francisco Bay Guardian, Boston's Weekly Dig and Portland's own Mix magazine. In 2000, she created Topaz Design. She also teaches at PNCA.

Kristen Dicharry Travis........ *page 42*
www.firesigndesign.com
kris@firesigndesign.com
After earning her B.F.A. in Multimedia Design at the University of Oregon, Kris Travis moved to (and fell in love with) Portland, where she established Firesign Design: print + web + identity + display.

97

DESIGNER CREDITS

Veronika Buck Valentova...... page 14
www.grafikalaveronika.com
veeva@seznam.cz
I am a young graphic designer, living between Portland and Prague, Czech Republic. I have over four years' experience in the fields of corporate identity, logo design, print design and web design.

Stephanie Vastakis................. page 73
Graphic Designer
www.stephanievastakis.com
s.vastakis@gmail.com
For me Graphic Design is many things. It's both my outlet and means of transforming my ideas into something tangible. I enjoy the problem-solving inherent in it and the opportunity to create something original. But mostly, I just like to make things.

Wendell Scott Walker........... page 66
http://issuu.com/wend/docs
Wendell Walker is not a man to be taken lightly. He is a photographer, printmaker, graphic designer and sometimes — when the moonlight's just right — a poet. His strength is born of true love and dogged wonderment and that is why there's no stopping him.

Waltronic Press.............. pages 20, 74
www.waltronic.net
waltronicpress@gmail.com
Waltronic Press is a printmaking studio that makes posters and T-shirts with an environmental focus. Each design calls for a ton of activism, a gallon of ink, a cup of imagination, and a dash of propaganda. Waltronic Press: Design, Make, Change.

Gail Weiss ....page 55
http://phantomchicken.com
gail@phantomchicken.com
503.233.4971
Since 2000, I've been doing graphic design and pre-press for our mom & pop shop: Phantom Chicken Screen Printing located right here in Portland, Oregon. I also enjoy paper collage and sewing to maintain a constant positive creative flow.

James Wigger........................ page 49
www.jameswigger.com
503 806 2852
Photographer / Graphic Designer / Polaroider / font lover / texturizer / plastic camera aficionado

Nonnie Wong.......................... page 31
www.coroflot.com/nonnie
nonnie.n3@gmail.com
Working happily as a communication designer at Ziba Design. Please contact for more info.

FOUNDER / EDITOR CREDITS

About the founder // Melissa Delzio

designed page 23, cover, and rest of book

Our Portland Story is an independent creative venture spearheaded by Portland freelance designer, Melissa Delzio. With this project, Melissa seeks to create a greater sense of community identity and pride in Portland and to capture the spirit of the city.

Melissa Delzio is a freelance graphic designer and creative entrepreneur with over six years of experience producing print and web graphics for international and local consumer brands alike. Professionally, Melissa strives to evolve the greater creative community she is a part of. Through serving on the Board of Directors for AIGA Portland (the professional association for design), she actively works to strengthen the local Portland design scene.

Melissa Delzio was born in the sweltering Colorado River town of Lake Havasu City, Arizona. After 18 sunburned years of the big Arizona sky, windswept sand dunes, and palm trees, Melissa started her journey north. She settled for four years in the quaint Route 66 hippie town of Flagstaff, Arizona, where she obtained her BFA degree in Visual Communication from Northern Arizona University. Melissa journeyed farther north to Portland, Oregon, in 2004. Upon arrival, Melissa quickly fell into a designer position at a small firm and set about making Portland home. Five years later, Melissa is a full-blown esplanade-jogging, NPR-listening, Pinot Noir-drinking, art-obsessed Portlander. She is an overzealous recycler and can sing the entire Greek Alphabet.

To learn more about Melissa, visit **www.meldel.com.**

About the editor // Sarah Koch

Sarah Koch, aka Julia Sarah Koch, is a second - (on her father's side) and third - (on her mother's) generation Portlander. Not surprisingly, she has a deep affection for — some would say a mild obsession with — all things Portland.

By the age of 12, Sarah had already revealed a tendency towards nit-pickiness that would earn her both friends and enemies. Even so, it took her a couple of decades to recognize and accept her true calling as a proofreader and copyeditor. Once she did, however, the days of riding the rails and living a carefree existence ended. (That last sentence is made up. She never rode the rails, nor has she ever been particularly carefree.)

Her life as a freelance proofreader, copyeditor, researcher, and writer has proved very satisfying. As a writer, she may be most proud of her "A Henry James Filmography," an ongoing project first published in the *Henry James Review* (Fall 1998), that melded her love of James with international TV and big screen adaptations of his work. Both the love affair and the resulting project came to life while Sarah was earning an MA in literature at Portland State University.

Currently, besides her regular work and — joyously — volunteering as editor to Our Portland Story, she is working on a series of suspense novels built around a character suspiciously similar to the author, set in Portland and the surrounding area. As anyone reading OPS can tell, this town has a rich history and a remarkable character for any author to draw upon.

Acknowledgments

I would like to thank all the authors and designers who contributed their stories and talents to the making of this book. Additionally, there are many people/organizations who helped make this book a reality.

Thanks to Andrew Barden and Ron Eddy, two developers who worked long hours getting the OurPortlandStory.com up and running in time for the launch. Thanks to Arran Stokes who volunteered his time to help with project management and event planning. Thanks to AIGA Portland — the professional association for design — who helped get designers involved with the project.

In addition, I would like to dedicate this book to Roberta Tsuboi, who contributed the story on page 30. Roberta (Robbie) passed away in early 2010. She was a former co-worker and friend of mine, but more importantly, she was a Portlander dedicated to making the Portland community better. By day she was a bookkeeper, by night she would devote her time to one of her many charity side-projects. From the swing band, to the food shelter, to the youth groups, Robbie put her time and energy into making others feel important and valued. Never have I a met a woman with such a generous (and active) soul and the ripple effects from her work will continue to be seen and felt in Portland for decades to come.

On a personal note, I would like to thank my beau, Ryan, for being incredibly supportive of this project. His proofreading, spreading fliers, brainstorming, and making dinner, helped keep me sane and well-fed through this process. A final thanks to my wonderful parents who instilled in me confidence, drive, the importance of creativity, and a love of extra marinara sauce.

THANK YOU ALL,
- Melissa Delzio

Never imagined I'd live here. Couldn't ask for PDX much more. PDX iz THE place to be!
~Ryan S.

Dear Portland,
I thought I would only live here for a few years, but I fell in love. Thank you for being so incredible.

Portland — yes sir / ma'am / ma'am / I came to all for it & now twelve years ob. Can't show me the one. Can totally followed it because it was at NYC — which was 1) Not at dreaming of me at back it. Let's encourage shot. I'm for moon of shot. Welcome your moon endurance. info

PDX, BABY...
I'm so glad I got to know you. I'm so glad I got to know you. As soon as you learn to stop hanging out with hipsters while drinking PBR tall boys, we'll be BFF. (I'm sure surf well be BFF. Hope you have a great summer this year -- PLEASE!
Love ya -- Kari

Thank you for year helpful hour been awesome bottom you truly rock. Gift Kit